P9-DMH-336

Martha Stewart's
QUICK COOK ™

Martha Stewart's
QUICK COOK ™

Photographs by Michael Geiger
Designed by Roger Black

Clarkson N. Potter, Inc./Publishers NEW YORK
DISTRIBUTED BY CROWN PUBLISHERS, INC.

*To my mother, Martha Kostyra, and
her mother,
my early teachers*

*Photographs copyright © 1983 by Michael Geiger
Recipes copyright © 1983 by Martha Stewart*

*All rights reserved. No part of this book may be reproduced or
transmitted in any form or by any means, electronic or mechanical,
including photocopying, recording, or by any information storage and
retrieval system, without permission in writing from the publisher.*

*Published by Clarkson N. Potter, Inc.,
225 Park Avenue South, New York, New York 10003*

QUICK COOK is a trademark of House Beautiful *Magazine, The Hearst Corporation*

Manufactured in Japan

Library of Congress Cataloging-in-Publication Data

*Stewart, Martha
Martha Stewart's Quick cook.*

*1. Cookery.   2. Menus.   I. Title.   II. Title: Quick cook.
TX652.S73   1983   641.5'55   83-13916
ISBN 0-517-55096-2*

16 15 14 13 12

Acknowledgments

I would like very much to thank the following people for their contributions to *Quick Cook*.

For their help in the kitchen and in the developing and creating of recipes, and in the actual styling of food, my warmest appreciation and thanks to Sara Foster, one of America's great young chefs; Jane Stacey, an accomplished, creative pastry chef and individualistic cook; Lisa Krieger, an original cook and very educated stylist and flower designer; Dana Munro, a hard-working organizer and stylist; Susan Ward, a young caterer with lots of new ideas; and Dorian Parker for her wealth of knowledge about all things culinary and otherwise.

To my dear friends who opened their numerous cupboards and drawers when mine were finally empty of props for the pictures: Naiad Einsel, Suzy Schwartz, Dana Munro, Maxine Krieger, and Lisa Krieger.

To Betsy Dickey for keeping the phone calls and office work organized while we photographed and wrote. To Necy Fernandes for keeping my house in order even though we used almost every room as a "studio" during the photography.

To Anne de Ravel for testing and coordinating the recipes for the book.

To Ruth Leserman for her extraordinary inventiveness.

To Michael Geiger, who photographed the menus for *Quick Cook*. His work is art, and the care and pain and pleasure that went into each photograph is certainly evident in the final product.

To my friend Roger Black for designing my second book. His work is clear and pure and highly complements the photography.

To the wonderful people at Clarkson Potter: especially my hard working editor Carolyn Hart, and associate editor Kathy Powell, Michael Fragnito, and art director Gael Dillon.

To Joann Barwick and Betty Boote at *House Beautiful* magazine for their help in planning the book.

To my husband, Andy, for tasting all the *Quick Cook* recipes.

Contents

Acknowledgments 5
Introduction 9

Spring

Rack of Baby Lamb with Herb Crust 15
Angel Hair with Broccoli 19
Grilled Veal Chops with Mustard-Herb Butter 23
Omelette with Wild Mushrooms 27
Chicken Paillard 30
Pan-Sautéed Trout Stuffed with Sage 35
Caramelized Pork Chops with Walnuts and Raisins . . . 39
Roast Leg of Lamb with Pan-Roasted Vegetables 43
Individual Pizzas 47
Saffron-Broiled Chicken Quarters 51
Assorted Wursts and Mustards 55
Seafood Salad 59
Broiled Salmon Steaks 63
Veal Scallopine alla Marsala 67

Summer

Spicy Lobster with Linguine 71
Grilled Butterflied Squabs with Mustard Sauce 75
Tortellini with Butter and Parmesan Cheese 79
Halibut with Fennel 83
Chicken Salad with Snow Peas and Water Chestnuts . . . 87
Steamed Shellfish with Herbs 91
Grilled Red Snapper with Tarragon Butter 95
Soft-Shell Crabs 99
Thyme-Sautéed Pork Chops with Apple Slices 103
Shrimp Chinoise 107
Red Snapper Baked in Parchment 111
Salad Niçoise à la Middlefield 115

Fall

Frittata 119

Sesame Chicken in Acorn Squash 123

Sole with Black Butter and Capers 127

Lamb Chops with Mint Butter 131

Pork Chops with Fennel 135

Smoked Turkey and Stilton Sandwiches 139

Crusty Mustard Chicken 142

Mussels with Pesto 147

Roast Pheasant 151

Sea Scallops Sautéed with Scallions 155

Grilled Breast of Duck 159

Pan-Fried Fillet of Beef 163

Spinach Soufflé 166

Winter

Broiled Steak with Béarnaise Sauce 171

Kielbasa Simmered in Beer and Onions 175

Shrimp Tortillas 179

Rotelle with Bacon and Sautéed Walnuts 183

Grilled Fillet of Beef with Black Peppercorns 187

Fillet of Sole Wrapped in Spinach 191

Fettuccine with Smoked Salmon and Fresh Peas 195

Oven-Braised Ham Steak 199

Mahagony Fried Chicken 203

Veal Piccata 207

Fried Oyster Sandwiches 211

Beef Liver with Sage 215

Herb-Roasted Chicken with Baked Shallots 219

Index 222

Foreword

*W*HEN YOU ARE MARRIED TO someone who cooks as well as my wife does, you pay more than the usual attention to the food you eat. I realize that I actually eat five different kinds of dinners: elaborate, many-course meals that Martha prepares for dinner-party guests; leftovers from Martha's catering parties; scrambled eggs that I can do myself; restaurant meals; and *Quick Cook* family dinners. I like *Quick Cook* dinners best. They're not expensive; they're fresh; and they're delicious.

Our house is never more inviting than when Martha has set the table for an inspired dinner to be created from what seems to be only a scattering of ingredients drawn from a nearly empty refrigerator and pantry. She seems to fly through the preparations to which I occasionally contribute my own poor chopping, scraping, and stirring skills.

I have eaten all of the *Quick Cook* meals described in this book at least once and most of them, or variations of them, many times. Some of them, like pork chops sautéed with thyme, frittata, and chicken paillard, have become as familiar as my favorite books on our library shelves. Potato slices sautéed in olive oil and sliced tomatoes with mozzarella and basil are as basic a food in our house as chicken soup was in my grandmother's kitchen.

The thought and effort that Martha has invested in the creation of *Quick Cook* will enrich the meals we look forward to at home and, I hope, through the publication of this book, the meals enjoyed by many other families.

Westport, Connecticut
May 30, 1983

Andrew Stewart

Introduction

❧

. . . .

QUICK COOK *BEGAN AS A* kind of game for me several years ago when I was a stockbroker on Wall Street. My daughter, Alexis, was very young and always hungry. My husband, Andy, was working as a lawyer then and was hungry for dinner the moment he got home from the office. When I returned home from work at five or six in the afternoon, I was faced with the daily challenge of feeding them interesting, varied meals. I lived as I envisioned a Parisian working woman lived, with an almost empty, but carefully inventive pantry and with an eye for what was fresh and inviting in the market. I never got into the habit of freezing casseroles or fresh meats and fishes for future thawing. I never bought an unripe tomato with the idea that it would be ready to eat in five days.

My "game" became more serious as the demands on my time increased. I formulated a formal set of *Quick Cook* rules to which I tried very hard to adhere: (1) to spend as little time as possible shopping, (2) to create mouth-watering, nutritious, healthful meals in a matter of minutes, (3) to see how and if I could simplify my favorite recipes, (4) to set a lovely, unusual table in a very short time, (5) to spend as little as possible on ingredients for each meal without sacrificing quality, (6) to re-invent, or re-create, for myself, the easiest, best ways for cooking foods, (7) to use as few utensils and pots and pans as possible.

I was brought up in a large family where meal preparation was often an all day affair—inexpensive cuts of meats were braised or stewed to make them more palatable. Vegetables were not necessarily fresh, but often had been canned by mother or grandmother the previous season. Cakes and pies were complicated, delicious concoctions, involving yeasts and fruit butters and rich frostings. Meals were more time consuming and the family spent more time together around the kitchen table. It was lovely, but everything was different then.

The philosophy of *Quick Cook* is the opposite of old-fashioned home cooking. *Quick Cook* takes fine-quality ingredients, impeccably fresh, and turns them into delightful, thoughtful meals with a minimum of fuss, concern, and time. Meals are generally prepared by portion, rather than measurement, which is more economical because there are no leftovers. The proportions of ingredients are flexible and are dictated by one's own particular taste and appetite. *Quick Cook* is very appropriate for family meals, small dinner parties, or just dinner for one or two.

Quick Cook is the solution for good cooks who have to deal with a busy work schedule yet desire to serve exceptional food to family and friends with a modicum of effort. My family and I don't tire of *Quick Cook* meals because the combinations, the variety, and the challenges are limitless.

Quick Cook uses five basic types of preparation: *steaming, grilling, sautéing, roasting* and *baking, broiling.* It relies only infrequently on *frying.*

Steaming is an extremely easy cooking technique to master. It requires, for ease, layered Oriental bamboo or metal steaming pans, and a very large, heavy frying pan or wok to contain the steamer and the water over which everything will cook. Timing is the important factor in steam cookery—everything cooks in less time than one would anticipate, and the shifting of the various steaming "layers" is extremely important if one desires perfectly cooked food. Steamers are excellent "portion" cookers, as shown in the steamed shellfish with herbs menu, where each layer contains one person's whole main course. It is also a very economical way to cook various vegetables—one needs only one steamer and one pan to cook large quantities and varieties.

Grilling over a fire in a fireplace, on a gas grill in your kitchen, on a grill in the yard, or over a campfire is certainly one of the easiest and most natural ways to cook a great variety of foods. Most of the recipes which call for grilling can be adapted to the broiler, but the flavors imparted to the meats and vegetables will not and cannot be the same. In the past year I have been experimenting with wet and dry marinades for grilled meats and fishes and herb-flavored butters, oils, and vinegars for vegetables and shellfish. Many of these recipes can be found in this book. I have also experimented with different woods, charcoals, and even old apples, corncobs, branches of dried and fresh herbs, and clippings from the berry patches to "flavor" the fire and smoke over which we cook. For fireplace cooking I have adapted an old, large oval hibachi with a new grill top in which to build the fire. This way my fireplaces remain cleaner (the coals are contained in the hibachi) and the heat can be more controlled. A Jenn-aire or other type of gas-fired grill is excellent, although you cannot obtain the more aromatic flavors of the wood or charcoal fires.

Radiant grilling, on a spit "in front of a fire" rather than over it, is another fascinating way to cook meats. In Switzerland I remember eating succulent lamb cooked by radiant heat. The meat, in this case a rack of young lamb, was spit roasted over a long metal dripping pan. The meat drippings were used to baste the meat, which was cooked to perfection in front of the great hot flaming fire behind it.

Whether you choose to grill over coals or in front of hot flames, some practice and experimentation is necessary. However, once you master the techniques, the results will be most satisfactory.

Sautéing is the basic, old-fashioned French way to *Quick Cook.* A small amount of oil and/or butter is heated until bubbling in a heavy skillet, and meat or fish, often lightly dredged in flavored flour, is very quickly cooked until golden in color. This method is excellent for thinly sliced fillets or scallops. I like to keep the fish or meat in rather small pieces for easy handling and extra-quick cooking. Well-flavored, easy sauces can be made right in the same pan by deglazing the pan with wine or fruit juice.

Roasting or *baking* is generally used for larger cuts of meat and for whole chickens, game birds, and fancy cuts of meat such as rack of lamb. I use roasting for vegetable tians—layered casseroles of thinly sliced vegetables —the variety of which is infinite. I bake huge, fluffy frittatas in a hot oven and high, light soufflés. The main rule for roasting or baking is that the oven must be *preheated* to the appropriate temperature *before* placing the food in it. *Braising* is basically roasting in a moderate oven, in a covered casserole.

Broiling is the fifth basic *Quick Cook* method. I use a Garland restaurant range for my family cooking, and it has an excellent broiler that is open to the air. I find that for steaks and thick chops most small home broilers tend to "steam" rather than broil. It is very important to preheat the broiler before inserting the food. Broil the food in a hot broiler, and regulate the cooking by adjusting the distance of the food from the flame rather than adjusting the flame. It is a bit tricky to get used to broiling, but as in other methods, a bit of practice is necessary for the finest results.

Frying is not one of my favored ways of cooking, although several of my family's favorite dishes are fried. For the most part I feel the results achieved by frying are oily, fattening, and generally less flavorful than other modes of cooking. However, good fried chicken is a way of life, and carefully prepared it can be fantastic. French fried potatoes, if prepared with good, perfectly sliced potatoes and excellent oil, are another culinary treat. I also enjoy eating whole Cornish hens that have been stuffed with aromatic herbs and deep fried in light cooking oil until crispy brown on the outside and juicy and succulent within.

The fifty-two menus in this book are arranged seasonally, as much for aesthetics as for the general availability of ingredients. Because of excellent shipping, we are often able to purchase unusual or hard-to-find fruits and vegetables "out of season," making the *Quick Cook's* job simpler because the shopping is easier.

The menus are designed to be cooked in an hour or less. When I say an hour, I mean that I really am cooking for an hour. I read each menu carefully beforehand, accomplish the shopping and gathering of ingredients, and get organized before I actually begin to cook. I make sure the oven or broiler is preheated. If grilling, I first light the grill. If I am serving ice cream parfaits, I make them first so the ice cream will have a chance to harden. Organization is of utmost importance, and utilization of the time at hand very essential in making these menus work.

There are certain things that I make ahead of time and freeze, such as pie crusts, cookies, puff pastry, and all types of fresh pasta. They are there not to cheat but to give me flexibility in menu planning. Sometimes a quick and easy fruit pie is just what I want to end a meal; having a 12-inch pastry round in the freezer is a great help.

The pantry must be well and cleverly stocked—with the almost day to day introduction of new and delicious oils, vinegars, and condiments, a pantry is bound to change its character and contents. However, that too is what *Quick Cook* is all about—using both basic and nonbasic ingredients to create fabulous meals. My pantry is certainly more complex and interesting than it was ten years ago, and the meals themselves reflect new trends and ideas in food preparation.

You will notice that many of the recipes in *Quick Cook* call for fresh herbs—thyme, rosemary, oregano, marjoram, chives, coriander, tarragon, basil, sage, parsley, mint. Herbs impart a flavor and aroma to foods that cannot be duplicated in any other way, and they are so easy to grow, both indoors and outdoors. If you cannot grow them yourself, make sure you have a good source for purchasing fresh herbs, and keep what you need in the refrigerator.

I invite you to read the following menus, try what appeals to you, and don't forget . . . set a beautiful table while the veal chops are grilling!

The Quick Cook's Pantry

Oils: light olive (I use Berio or Colavita), green olive, sesame (dark Oriental), walnut, almond, blended vegetable, peanut, hot chili, safflower

Vinegars: red wine, white wine, Japanese rice wine, balsamic or sherry, tarragon, raspberry, chili pepper, Champagne, cider

Dried pastas: linguine, fusilli (curly noodles), fettuccine, angel hair, spaghetti, buckwheat noodles, rotelle, orzo

Baking needs: unbleached flour, whole-wheat flour, rolled oats, cornmeal, granulated sugar, brown sugar, confectioners' sugar, honey, molasses, vanilla beans, vanilla extract, mint extract, powdered espresso, cocoa, baking chocolate (unsweetened and semisweet), semisweet chocolate chips, baking powder, salt, parchment paper, almond paste, candied ginger

Nuts and seeds: walnuts, almonds, hazelnuts, pecans, pine nuts, sesame seeds

Canned goods: anchovies, cornichons, olives, water chestnuts, black currants or blackberries, chicken and beef stock, tomatoes (plum and paste), sun-dried tomatoes (San Remo *pumate*), black beans, soy sauce (light and dark), Coco Lopez (coconut cream), sesame paste, chili paste, currant jelly, apricot jam, apple jelly, peanut butter, pineapple juice

Dried goods: flageolets (dried French beans), white long-grain rice, wild rice, Arborio rice (Italian rice), brown rice, dried mushrooms (porcini, cèpes, morels, Shitake), dried fruits, cat chow, doggie bones

Herbs and spices: coarse salt, peppercorns, cayenne pepper, chili powder, curry powder, red pepper flakes, bay leaves, celery seeds, paprika, cumin, saffron (ground and whole), ground cinnamon, cinnamon sticks, ground ginger, whole nutmeg, coriander, mace, whole cloves, allspice, star anise, cream of tartar

Wines and liquors: white wine, Sauterne, Marsala, Dubonnet, dry sherry, Cognac, Grand Marnier, Cointreau, coffee-flavored liqueur, crème de cassis, blackberry liqueur, kirsch, crème de menthe, Sambuca, vermouth, rum (light and dark), tequila, bourbon, scotch, vodka, several types of beer

The Quick Cook's Freezer

Pastry dough, yeast, pasta (ravioli, tortellini, fettuccine), puff pastry, rolls, breads, tortillas, pesto, ice creams and sorbets, frozen breast of duck, raisins (golden and muscat), bread crumbs, poppyseeds, wedges of Gorgonzola or Roquefort cheese, petit pois (baby peas), spinach, cranberries, cherries, raspberries, blueberries, homemade stocks, bacon, pancetta (Italian bacon), unsalted butter

❧

The Quick Cook's Refrigerator

Swiss cheese or Gruyère, several types of mustards, horseradish, Parmesan cheese for grating, piece of fresh ginger, lemons, limes, oranges, grapefruits, scallions, parsley, dill, heavy cream, unsalted butter, eggs, sour cream, crème fraîche, carrots, celery, orange juice, milk

❧

The Quick Cook's Vegetable Bin

Garlic, onions (red, white, yellow), shallots, potatoes (baking and red bliss)

Spring

❧

Rack of Baby Lamb
with Herb Crust

THERE ARE A LOT OF QUESTIONS concerning baby lamb—what is it really, does it even exist in the markets, is it available only in the spring, etc. A good butcher can generally provide you with genuine baby racks of lamb if you give him enough notice. I prefer really small racks—a seven-rib portion should weigh about 1 3/4 pounds at the most before trimming. I trim each rack myself so that there are no errors. I leave the rib bones longish and trim away excess fat from the bones, all the way to the eye of the rack. A good rack should be very firm—if the meat is falling away from the bones, or if the meat is too fatty, it will not make a lovely presentation. I do have the butcher carefully saw through the bottom of the rack so that carving it into individual chops will be easy. Leave about 1/4 inch of fat on the outside of the rack to keep the meat moist during roasting. Allow at least two chops per person.

This is one of my more formal *Quick Cook* menus, but actually one of the quickest to prepare. I serve the lamb with an herbed bread-crumb crust, fresh early spring asparagus, and a typical French accompaniment, stewed flageolets. The vegetables are chosen for their small size and presented in the way I like best—whole. Baby white turnips are carefully peeled, but the roots and tops are left intact. Asparagus of small size need no peeling and are steamed for a few minutes until tender. The flageolets, small, pale green French beans, are mixed with red runner beans.

In the spring you will begin to find blackberries in the market. Mixed with crème fraîche, a bit of sugar, and crème de cassis, they make a delicious blackberry fool dessert.

Note: Dried beans cook much more quickly when soaked overnight in cold water. However, when I haven't had time to do this, I have also had success boiling the beans in lightly salted water until tender (about 20 to 30 minutes) and then proceeding with the recipe.

The formal parlor in our house is the setting for this elegant yet extremely simple spring dinner (opposite). A nineteenth-century Japanese celadon platter holds the lamb and vegetables. After dinner Andy and I frequently like to relax with dessert (above) in another room of the house. The color of the delicate blackberry fool is enhanced by a bouquet of sweet Williams from the garden.

❧

MENU
Rack of Baby Lamb with Herb Crust
Steamed Asparagus
Baby Turnips
Flageolets and Red Runner Beans
Blackberry Fool

Rack of Baby Lamb with Herb Crust

SERVES 2 TO 3

> 1 rack of baby lamb (generally 7 chops)
> 1 cup fresh white-bread crumbs
> 1/2 cup finely chopped parsley or chervil
> 1 clove garlic, minced
> 2 tablespoons Dijon mustard
> 2 tablespoons olive oil
> 1 teaspoon salt
> Freshly ground pepper to taste

1. Preheat the oven to 400°. Carefully trim the rack of lamb, leaving the rib bones as long as possible. Leave about 1/4 inch of fat on the outside of the rack. Cut neat crisscrosses in the fat with a sharp knife.

2. In a small mixing bowl combine all the remaining ingredients.

3. Put the rack of lamb in a roasting pan and cook it in the oven for 15 minutes. Remove the lamb and reduce heat to 375°.

4. Pat the bread-crumb mixture on top of the rack and on the bony side to form a crust. Return to the oven for another 10 to 15 minutes. The lamb should be served very pink.

Steamed Asparagus

SERVES 2 TO 3

> 12 to 20 asparagus spears (allow 6 fat spears or 8 to 10 thin ones per person)
> 1 tablespoon unsalted butter
> Salt and pepper to taste

1. Trim asparagus (peel spears if they are fat) and put them in the top of a steamer over boiling water. Steam for 2 to 3 minutes if asparagus are thin, 5 to 6 minutes if fat.

2. Remove the asparagus from steamer and dot with butter. Season with salt and pepper and serve as a first course or with the lamb.

Baby Turnips

SERVES 2 TO 3

> 6 to 12 baby turnips
> 3 tablespoons unsalted butter
> 1/2 teaspoon sugar
> Salt and pepper to taste

1. Peel the turnips, leaving 1 to 2 inches of the green tops attached.

2. Put the turnips in a small saucepan with butter and sugar. Add enough water to barely cover and cook for 6 to 12 minutes, depending on their size, until tender. Drain, season lightly with salt and pepper, and serve.

❧

Flageolets and Red Runner Beans

SERVES 3

3 shallots, finely chopped
1 clove garlic, peeled and minced
3 tablespoons unsalted butter
1/2 pound of dried beans (a
    combination of flageolets and
    red runner beans), soaked
    overnight in cold water
1 bay leaf
2 or 3 sprigs fresh thyme
Salt and pepper to taste

1. Sauté shallots and garlic in butter. Add the presoaked beans and cover with cold water. Add bay leaf, thyme, and salt and pepper.

2. Bring to a boil, reduce the heat to a simmer, and cook for 45 to 55 minutes, or until beans are tender. Add water if necessary, but as the beans become tender let most of the water evaporate. Serve hot.

❧

Blackberry Fool

SERVES 2 TO 3

CRÈME FRAÎCHE (Makes 1 cup)

1 tablespoon buttermilk or sour
    cream
1 cup heavy cream

1/2 pint fresh blackberries
2 tablespoons sugar
    Dash of crème de cassis or
    framboise liqueur

1. To make crème fraîche, if not store bought, add buttermilk or sour cream to heavy cream. Mix and let sit at room temperature 6 to 8 hours. Cover and refrigerate at least 24 hours before using.

2. Set aside 6 to 9 of the prettiest berries. Put the rest of the berries and the remaining ingredients in a bowl and whip with an electric mixer at medium speed, or by hand with a wire whisk, until stiff. Do not overwhip, or the fool will become runny.

3. Spoon into glasses and chill until ready to serve. Decorate with the reserved whole berries.

Angel Hair with Broccoli

Pasta, in all its many variations, is one of the easiest Quick Cook meals of all. I always have some on hand, either dried or fresh, in the freezer. In combination with a colorful vegetable like broccoli, it makes a nutritious and satisfying meal in minutes. A nineteenth-century Wedgwood creamware plate is used for the main course and a new Wedgwood drabware plate for the braised escarole and broccoli rabe. The table is covered with a mat made from a Japanese obi, an idea I got from my sister-in-law Diane Love.

MENU
Angel Hair with Broccoli
Braised Escarole and Broccoli Rabe
Hot Garlic Bread
Vanilla Ice Cream Sambuca and Amaretti Cookies

*S*PRING IS A SEASON OF CON-
tradictions. Days may be warm and sunny one week and cold and wintry
the next. We may be tempted with giant strawberries in the market one day
and the next be told that heavy rains have wiped out the crops in California.
But a few vegetables, like broccoli, always seem to be on hand in the supermarkets, and a very pleasing, simple meal can be concocted with them in
combination with pasta.

Escarole, typical of a hardy winter lettuce with its yellow-green leaves
and curly edges, is delicious in salads with a hot bacon dressing, or braised
as in this menu with broccoli rabe, another green vegetable that appears in
February and March.

❧

Angel Hair with Broccoli
SERVES 4

1 **bunch fresh broccoli**
   Salt to taste
1/4 **cup light olive oil**
4 **tablespoons (1/2 stick) unsalted**
   butter
2 **scallions, cut into 1/4-inch pieces**
1 **clove garlic, peeled and crushed**
2 **tablespoons white wine**
1 **pound angel-hair pasta**
   Grated Parmesan cheese to taste

1. Cut broccoli into flowerets. Peel and chop the stem into bite-size
pieces.

2. Cook the broccoli in lightly salted boiling water for 3 to 4 minutes until
crispy but tender. Drain and place in ice water to cool. Drain.

3. In a saucepan heat oil and 3 tablespoons butter over medium heat.

4. In a skillet melt remaining 1 tablespoon butter and sauté the scallions
and garlic for 2 minutes. Add the wine and cook for 5 minutes. Add melted
butter and oil, then the blanched broccoli. Heat thoroughly.

5. Cook the pasta in a large pot of salted boiling water until *al dente,* about
30 seconds (angel hair cooks very quickly). Drain well and put in a serving
dish. Toss with the broccoli mixture. Serve at once with Parmesan cheese.

Braised Escarole and Broccoli Rabe

SERVES 4

> 1 pound fresh broad-leaf escarole
> 1 pound broccoli rabe
> 1/4 cup light olive oil
> 4 tablespoons (1/2 stick) unsalted
>   butter
> 2 cloves garlic, peeled and crushed
> 4 scallions, chopped
>   Salt and pepper to taste
>   Lemon wedges

1. Wash escarole and broccoli rabe. Dry well. Trim the broccoli rabe and tear the leaves of escarole into 4-inch pieces.

2. In a sauté pan, heat the oil and melt the butter over low heat. Add scallions and garlic and cook gently for 5 minutes, but do not brown.

3. Add the escarole and broccoli rabe. Toss while cooking over medium-high heat until vegetables are wilted, about 3 minutes. Season to taste with salt and pepper. Serve hot with lemon wedges.

Hot Garlic Bread

SERVES 4

> 1 loaf French or Italian bread
> 4 or 5 cloves garlic, peeled and
>   sliced lengthwise
> 4 tablespoons olive oil

1. Preheat oven to 350°. Cut bread into diagonal slices 1 inch thick and rub each slice on both sides with the cut garlic.

2. Brush the slices lightly with olive oil and put them on a baking sheet. Toast in the oven until crispy, turning once. Serve immediately.

Vanilla Ice Cream Sambuca

SERVES 4

Spoon vanilla ice cream into parfait glasses or goblets, pour 2 tablespoons Sambuca Romana over each serving, and dust with powdered espresso coffee. Serve with amaretti (Italian macaroons).

Grilled Veal Chops with Mustard-Herb Butter

*T*HIS IS THE FIRST OF MANY *Quick Cook* menus that may or may not be cooked almost entirely on a grill. Purchase the thickest, palest veal chops you can find and grill them, if you can, over hot coals of mesquite wood with leeks and red onions. The chops are brushed once or twice during grilling with a mustard-herb butter, which is also used to flavor the leeks and onions. (If a grill is not easily available, you can broil the chops and vegetables in a hot broiler.)

The blackened leeks would be too tough to eat if the leeks were not first poached in salted water for about 10 minutes, drained, and then grilled. The red onions, peeled and quartered, soften nicely over the coals without prior cooking.

For dessert try stewed rhubarb. The long red stalks of this unusual fruit are commonly available in groceries from the middle of March (Florida rhubarb) through June, when the local crops are proliferating. I have two long rows of rhubarb plants in the garden, and this year I'm planting a third because so many people are asking for rhubarb desserts—pies, tarts, and custards, or just plain stewed rhubarb, served as in this menu, with spoonfuls of crème fraîche. Rhubarb is very easy to grow. Buy strong select roots of an everbearing type. Try to purchase a variety that is red, sweet, stringless, and hardy; New Valentine or Crimson Red are two types with which I've had success. Plant as a border or in a row where the plants will not be disturbed. A rhubarb patch lasts for years and years. Remember that the leaves of rhubarb, like the leaves of tomatoes, are poisonous.

Note: Mesquite wood is sold in hardware stores and gourmet shops and can also be ordered from mail-order food catalogs. Chunks or chips of mesquite should be added to a hot charcoal fire about a half hour before grilling.

In our newly reconstructed circa 1900 barn we have a huge brick and fieldstone fireplace, which is wonderful for warm fires on cool spring evenings. We often grill on an old hibachi in front of the fire; this way, there is no dripping of grease onto the floor. Old English brass and iron trivets hold kettles of water for tea and coffee.

MENU
Grilled Veal Chops with Mustard-Herb Butter
Blackened Leeks and Red Onions
Salad of Endive and Hot Walnuts
Stewed Rhubarb

Grilled Veal Chops with Mustard-Herb Butter

SERVES 2

2 veal chops, 1 1/2 inches thick

MUSTARD-HERB BUTTER

4 tablespoons (1/2 stick) unsalted butter, softened
1 1/2 tablespoons Dijon mustard
1 shallot, minced
1 tablespoon chopped parsley
1 tablespoon chopped chervil or tarragon
1 tablespoon chopped chives
Freshly ground pepper to taste

1. In a mixing bowl or food processor combine butter, mustard, shallot, parsley, chervil, chives, and pepper. Mix well and set aside (at room temperature).

2. Cook veal chops on a grill over hot coals, turning them every 2 minutes and brushing with the mustard-herb butter. (Save some herb butter for the vegetables. Check for doneness after 10 to 12 minutes; the veal should be light pink.

Note: The veal chops can also be cooked in a preheated hot broiler for 12 to 15 minutes. Turn every 4 to 5 minutes.

Blackened Leeks and Red Onions

SERVES 2

4 to 6 small leeks
2 tablespoons unsalted butter
1 teaspoon salt
2 large red onions, peeled and quartered

1. Trim and wash the leeks.

2. In a saucepan combine butter, salt, and enough water to cover the leeks. Bring to a boil and poach the leeks over medium-low heat for 10 minutes. Drain.

3. Put the leeks and onions over the hot coals and grill them for about 5 minutes, brushing with the mustard-herb butter, and using long tongs to turn the vegetables.

Salad of Endive and Hot Walnuts

SERVES 2

> 2 small heads endive
> 3 tablespoons walnut oil *
> 1/4 cup walnut pieces
> 1 1/2 tablespoons balsamic vinegar
> Salt and freshly ground pepper

1. Slice endive leaves into narrow strips and arrange them on individual plates.

2. In a skillet heat the oil and toast the walnuts until lightly browned. Stir in vinegar, pour over salad, season to taste, and serve immediately.

   * Olive oil can be substituted for walnut oil and any good red wine vinegar for the balsamic vinegar, but the flavor will be much milder.

Stewed Rhubarb

SERVES 2

> 1 pound rhubarb stalks
> 3/4 cup sugar, or to taste
> 1 tablespoon ground coriander
> Grated rind of 1 orange
> 2 tablespoons (1/4 stick) unsalted
>   butter
> Crème fraîche (see page 17)

1. Wash rhubarb and cut into 1/2-inch pieces. Put in a medium-size bowl, sprinkle with sugar, and let sit for at least 30 minutes.

2. Cook rhubarb in a saucepan over low heat until soft, 15 to 20 minutes. Taste for sweetness.

3. Stir in coriander, orange rind, and butter. Serve warm or at room temperature with crème fraîche.

Note: This will make more than 2 servings, but it can be kept in the refrigerator for several days. It is delicious for breakfast.

Omelette with Wild Mushrooms

WHENEVER I'M ASKED WHICH food I would choose to have on hand always, I answer without hesitation: eggs, fresh eggs. My mother-in-law has been after me for years to simplify my life a bit and "get rid of the chickens," but they are so much a part of the household that I could never bear to part with them. The chickens are all rare breeds, especially beautiful to look at. We keep about a hundred birds of various kinds—Cochins, Araucanas, Mottled Houdans, Polish, Brahmas, Speckled Sussex, and others too numerous to list—and they lay an extraordinary assortment of multihued eggs, which I use for my family, my friends, and the catering business. Crêpes are really more golden in color, pasta is more yellow, cakes are lighter and richer, madeleines puffier when we use our own eggs. And omelettes are fantastic!

This menu consists of one of my favorite meals: a mushroom-filled omelette, a platter of sautéed fennel and potatoes, a simple Boston lettuce salad (I also use greenhouse-grown mache, lamb's lettuce), pan-toasted French bread, and a satisfying yet very easy chocolate dessert.

The omelette is cooked to order, for it must be eaten immediately. Fresh eggs make the best omelettes (and the best poached eggs, for that matter). The white is thicker and the yolk heavier. I prefer 3 eggs for a main-course omelette and like generous amounts of fillings. If wild mushrooms are not available, try leafy spinach, creamed leeks, crab meat and shallots, finely chopped fresh herbs, grated Gruyère, or slivers of Brie as fillings.

A fluffy 3-egg omelette looks especially beautiful turned out onto a tortoise-shell-patterned English Majolica plate. An English trug basket holds an assortment of eggs.

MENU

Omelette with Wild Mushrooms
Pan-Sautéed Fennel and Potatoes
Boston Lettuce Salad
Pan-Toasted French Bread
Individual Chocolate Cake Trifles

Omelette with Wild Mushrooms

PER OMELETTE

2 tablespoons (1/4 stick) unsalted
   butter
1/4 cup fresh wild mushrooms
   (shitake, porcini, girolles,
   cèpes, etc.), sliced if large
   Salt and pepper to taste
2 or 3 fresh eggs
2 tablespoons clarified butter
   Fresh parsley or chervil, finely
   chopped, to taste

1. In a small skillet melt the butter and sauté the mushrooms for 3 to 4 minutes. Season with salt and pepper. Remove skillet from heat and keep mushrooms warm.

2. Lightly beat the eggs in a bowl with salt and pepper.

3. Heat the clarified butter in an omelette pan (8 inches in diameter for a 2-egg omelette, 9 inches for 3 eggs). When the butter is hot but not smoking, pour in the eggs. With a fork or a spatula pull them away from the sides of the pan while moving the pan back and forth across the flame constantly so the eggs do not stick. Lower the heat if necessary to let the eggs cook through without browning.

4. Just before the omelette is set, spoon the mushroom filling into the center, sprinkle with the chopped herb, and roll onto a warm serving plate.

Pan-Sautéed Fennel and Potatoes

SERVES 4

3/4 cup olive oil
4 to 6 fresh rosemary sprigs
2 large baking potatoes, peeled
   and cut into thin slices
2 medium fennel bulbs, cut into
   1/8-inch slices
   Salt and freshly ground pepper
   to taste

1. In a heavy skillet or wok, heat the oil until very hot but not smoking. Add the rosemary to the hot oil.

2. Fry the potatoes, stirring often, until golden. Remove potatoes with a slotted spoon and drain on paper towel.

3. Sauté the fennel slices in the same oil until tender and just browned around the edges. Drain on paper towel, mix with potatoes, and season.

Boston Lettuce Salad

SERVES 4

*Allow a handful of Boston
lettuce per serving*

LIGHT VINAIGRETTE DRESSING
(Makes ¾ cup)

6 tablespoons almond oil
*3 tablespoons champagne or white
  wine vinegar*
Pinch of sugar
Salt and pepper to taste
*Fresh chopped herbs (dill,
  coriander, chervil) to taste*

1. Arrange the lettuce on individual serving plates.

2. Whisk the oil into the vinegar; add sugar and salt and pepper. Sprinkle
dressing with herbs and drizzle over lettuce.

Pan-Toasted French Bread

For each serving, sauté 2 or 3 one-half-inch-thick slices of French or Italian
bread in 1 tablespoon melted, unsalted butter until golden, turning once.
Serve immediately.

Individual Chocolate Cake Trifles

SERVES 4

*1 pint strawberries
  Cognac or rum to taste*
1 tablespoon cocoa
1 cup heavy cream
*1 chocolate layer cake, 8 or 9
  inches in diameter, or 4
  serving-size pieces of leftover
  chocolate cake*

1. Hull and slice all but 4 berries, sprinkle with Cognac, and set aside.

2. Dissolve the cocoa with a little Cognac and set aside.

3. Whip the cream and set it aside.

4. Put several berry slices in the bottom of 4 parfait glasses. Crumble the
cake and cover the berries with some of the crumbs and sprinkle the cake
generously with Cognac mixture. Top with a dollop of whipped cream.
Repeat this layering of ingredients until the glass is filled. Top with whipped
cream and a whole berry, and chill. The trifle can be made several hours
before serving or the night before.

The table is set with hand-made linen placemats designed and woven by my daughter, Alexis, and illuminated by a grouping of Andy's kerosene lamps. We often use such lamps for dinner-table lighting and now collect them instead of candlesticks. If you keep the wicks long and clean, and the hurricanes washed, the light is lovely.

Chicken Paillard

✿

MENU
Chicken Paillard
Risotto with Porcini
Hot Salad of Escarole and Pancetta
Italian Flat Breads
Oranges in Red Wine

For dessert, fresh oranges are served with a sauce of red wine spiced with star anise, a licorice-flavored ingredient frequently used in Chinese cooking. They look especially lovely displayed on a glass pedestal cake stand. The gray vicuna cloth covering the table was also woven by Alexis.

𝒢RILLED OR BROILED PAILLARD of meat has become very popular with diet-conscious diners everywhere. In New York almost every good restaurant offers paillards of chicken, veal, or beef. The requirement is the same for all three—the meat must be of the highest quality, cut very thin, and, if necessary, pounded slightly so as to be of uniform thickness. Grilling is done immediately before serving, and the searing lines of the grill are apparent on the meat. The grill or broiler should be very hot; if a fire is being used, coals should be hot with no flames.

This menu offers an Italian risotto as a side dish for the paillard. The risotto must also be cooked right before serving. This one is flavored with porcini mushrooms. The rice used for risotto must be the short-grain Italian variety known as Arborio rice, which can be found in gourmet and specialty food shops. American rice will not do, since it does not have the sticky consistency of the Arborio.

Chicken Paillard

SERVES 4

> 2 whole chicken breasts, boned,
> skinned, and well chilled
> 2 tablespoons (1/4 stick) unsalted
> butter, melted
> Lemon wedges

1. Preheat the broiler or prepare a charcoal fire.

2. Remove all fat and sinew from the chicken breasts. With a sharp knife cut each breast crosswise into 2 pieces. Put each half between two sheets of wax paper and pound until very thin. Chill until ready to use.

3. Brush one side of each piece with melted butter and put under the broiler or over the coals. Grill for about 3 minutes. Turn chicken over and brush the other side with butter. The grill will sear the meat and leave some black lines. Serve immediately with lemon wedges.

❧

Risotto with Porcini

SERVES 4

> 8 to 12 fresh porcini mushrooms
> (or 1/2 ounce dried, plus 1/4
> cup warm white wine)
> 3 cups chicken stock
> 5 tablespoons unsalted butter
> 2 shallots, minced
> 1 1/2 cup Italian Arborio rice
> 1/2 cup freshly grated Parmesan
> cheese

1. Trim and clean mushrooms, then set aside. (If using dried mushrooms, soak them in wine for at least 1/2 hour.)

2. Bring stock to a boil. Reduce heat to keep stock at a low simmer.

3. In a heavy saucepan melt 3 tablespoons butter over medium heat and sauté the shallots for 5 minutes, or until translucent. Do not brown them. Add the rice, stir well to coat with butter. Raise heat and cook rice until opaque.

4. Stir in a cup of the simmering stock and cook until the rice has absorbed all the liquid, stirring constantly.

5. Add another 1/2 cup of stock and stir until all liquid has been absorbed. Add another 1/2 cup stock and repeat until all stock is used. At the end the rice should be neither dry nor soggy, but moist and creamy with a slight crunch. Stir constantly to avoid having rice stick to the bottom. The whole process should take 35 to 40 minutes.

6. If using dried mushrooms, drain them well. In a skillet melt the remaining butter and sauté the mushrooms (fresh or dried) for 2 minutes over medium-high heat. Add to the risotto. Serve at once with Parmesan cheese on the side.

Hot Salad of Escarole and Pancetta

SERVES 4

Allow a large handful of escarole per person

DRESSING (Makes 1 cup)

1/3 *cup pancetta (Italian bacon), or thick-sliced bacon, cut into 1/2-inch cubes*
1/3 *cup balsamic vinegar*
1/4 *cup light olive oil*
Salt and pepper to taste

1. Arrange the escarole in a large salad bowl.

2. Sauté the pancetta quickly in a hot skillet until slightly browned. Add vinegar and bring to a boil. Remove from the heat.

3. Stir in olive oil and season with salt and pepper. Pour immediately over the escarole, toss, and serve warm.

Oranges in Red Wine

SERVES 4

2 *cups red wine*
1/2 *cup sugar*
2 *star anise*
1 *tablespoon Grand Marnier (optional)*
4 *oranges*

1. Combine wine, sugar, and star anise in a saucepan. Bring to a boil, reduce heat, and simmer for about 10 minutes, or until reduced to 1 1/2 cups. Add the Grand Marnier. Set aside to cool.

2. Using a zester, make fine strips of the rinds of oranges. Add half the strips to the syrup and set the rest aside for garnish.

3. With a sharp paring knife peel all of the oranges. Remove all the white membrane, cutting as little of the pulp as possible. Arrange the oranges in a large bowl, or compote.

4. Pour the syrup over the oranges and garnish with the remaining zest. Serve at room temperature.

Pan-Sautéed Trout Stuffed with Sage

I have been collecting copper cookware for almost twenty years. This oval pan, just large enough to hold the trout, was purchased on one of my first trips to France with Andy. I try to use each copper pot at least once every three weeks, polishing it before hanging it back on the rack in the kitchen. The fish is accompanied by fresh red pepper pasta and a salad of endive and radicchio, a red Italian chicory that can be grown in the garden and is becoming increasingly available in markets.

MENU

Pan-Sautéed Trout Stuffed with Sage
Red Pepper Pasta with Red Pepper Strips and Parmesan
Endive and Radicchio Salad
Lemon Sorbet

*W*HEN I WAS A LITTLE GIRL I used to get up very early on cold Saturday mornings in spring, dress in layers of clothing, and ride on my old Schwinn bicycle with my brother, Eric, to our favorite trout stream. We'd fish all morning for speckled trout and bring it home to the family for supper that night. We would grill or sauté the fish, and I still think this is the best way to prepare it. I do like to stuff the fish with herbs, using sage, thyme, summer savory, dill, parsley, or combinations of many herbs. Each trout takes only a few minutes to cook, and the herbs impart a most delicate flavor to the flesh of the fish.

A simple salad of available spring greens (I am partial to radicchio and endive) is perfect.

Fresh pasta can be made in less than an hour, but I prefer to make it ahead and freeze it. Packed in rigid, airtight plastic containers, it keeps quite well in the freezer and is wonderful all year long. This unusual red pepper pasta was the invention of my friend Ruth Leserman, who is constantly coming up with unusual new pasta combinations. It is best when the bell peppers are large and very sweet. If you prefer a spicier pasta, you can add a fresh chili pepper to the dough.

Pan-Sautéed Trout Stuffed with Sage

SERVES 6

6 trout (boned, if desired, but left whole)
24 to 36 small sprigs fresh sage
Salt and pepper to taste
6 tablespoons (3/4 stick) unsalted butter
6 tablespoons safflower oil
Lemon wedges

1. Stuff each trout with 4 to 6 sprigs of herb, according to taste. Sprinkle with salt and pepper. Tie the trout with a bit of twine or butcher string to hold filling.

2. In a large sauté pan, or several smaller ones (all the trout should be cooked at the same time), heat the butter and oil. Sauté the trout over medium-high heat for 5 minutes. Turn and cook them for 5 more minutes. They may need a few additional minutes, depending on their thickness. Serve with lemon wedges.

Red Pepper Pasta with
Red Pepper Strips and Parmesan

SERVES 6

3 red bell peppers, seeded
1 hot chili pepper, seeded
    (optional)
1 egg yolk from a large egg
    Pinch of salt
    Pinch of cayenne pepper
3 to 4 cups all-purpose flour
    Cornmeal

SAUCE (Makes 1 cup)

6 tablespoons (3/4 stick) unsalted
    butter
2 tablespoons olive oil
2 red bell peppers, seeded and
    julienned into fine strips
2/3 cup of grated Parmesan (or
    Asiago) cheese
    Salt and pepper to taste

1. In a food processor, purée the red bell peppers and the chili pepper.

2. Add the egg yolk, salt, and cayenne pepper. Process until the mixture is smooth and there are no large pieces of pepper.

3. Add 1 1/2 cups flour and mix well. Continue adding the flour, 1/2 cup at a time, processing until the dough becomes stiff and smooth. The dough eventually will hold together and form a ball, coming away cleanly from the sides of the bowl. Remove the dough from the bowl. If it sticks to your hands, knead in some additional flour. Form a ball and place the dough under an overturned bowl so that it is kept covered.

4. Divide the dough into 1/2 cup amounts. Using a pasta machine (I use a hand-operated Italian machine), pass each piece through the widest setting. Reduce the setting by one notch and pass the dough through again. Repeat until you reach the desired thickness for the dough. Dry the broad pasta for a few minutes on a rack.*

5. Set the machine to fettuccine width and pass the broad noodles through it. Dust each batch with cornmeal to prevent the strips from sticking together. Put them on a baking sheet and cover. Do not allow the fresh pasta to dry out. Refrigerate, covered, until ready to use.

6. In a large pan, heat the butter and oil and sauté the pepper strips over medium-high heat for 4 to 5 minutes.

7. Bring a large pot of lightly salted water to a boil. Add the pasta and cook for 2 to 3 minutes, or until *al dente.* Fresh pasta cooks very quickly. Drain.

8. Toss the cooked pasta and the cheese with the sautéed peppers. Season with salt and pepper. Serve immediately.

* I use an old laundry rack for drying the pasta, but a broomstick placed between two chairs or the edge of an open drawer also works.

Caramelized Pork Chops
with Walnuts and Raisins

I AM OFTEN TEMPTED TO PUR-
chase vegetables or fruits that are totally out of season in our locale, but available in the supermarkets and green grocers. In the late winter and early spring months I can find plump green asparagus from Mexico and ripe juicy pineapples from Hawaii, mangoes from Haiti and baby string beans from Senegal. The following menu calls for both asparagus and pineapple, but if you have difficulty locating either, remember that flexibility is part of being a good and creative cook; substitutions in these menus are not only acceptable but often necessary. The orange butter served with the asparagus is a delicate concoction, a flavored sauce to which the butter is added until it is thick and creamy.

Choose pork chops that are at least one-inch thick and cut from the rib or loin, pale pink, and well trimmed of fat. They are marinated for a short time in sugar and cider vinegar, then the marinade is discarded and the chops are sautéed until they are a deep caramel color. Sherry, walnut oil, walnut halves, and raisins make the topping for the pork chops. Served with wild rice and a salad of winter endive and red onion, this is an unusual meal that is very simple to prepare.

A simple salad of endive and red onion looks especially inviting on an old Majolica plate. In contrast, the dinner is served on a plain, oversized white restaurant plate. A light-bodied Bordeaux wine would be perfect with this meal.

❧

MENU
Steamed Asparagus with Orange Butter
Caramelized Pork Chops with Walnuts and Raisins
Wild Rice
Salad of Endive and Red Onion
Fresh Pineapple and Coconut Curls

Steamed Asparagus with Orange Butter

SERVES 4

1 pound asparagus
1 orange
1 tablespoon Grand Marnier
1 tablespoon champagne or white
  wine vinegar
8 tablespoons (1 stick) cold
  unsalted butter

1. Trim and peel the asparagus. Peel the stems if asparagus are thick. Steam until just tender, about 4 to 5 minutes.

2. Squeeze the orange and strain the juice. Reserve both pulp and juice.

3. In a saucepan combine orange juice, Grand Marnier, and vinegar. Over medium heat reduce to 2 tablespoons. Remove from the heat and whisk the butter into the liquid, 1 tablespoon at a time, until well incorporated and mixture is thick and creamy. Do not reheat or butter will melt. If mixture becomes too thick, or butter refuses to soften, hold pan over simmering water to warm slightly.

4. Stir in the orange pulp and spoon the butter over the hot asparagus.

Caramelized Pork Chops with Walnuts and Raisins

SERVES 4

1/2 cup sugar
1/2 cup cider vinegar
4 pork chops, 1-inch thick
6 tablespoons vegetable oil
4 tablespoons walnut oil
1/2 cup walnut halves
1/4 cup dry sherry
1/2 cup raisins

1. In a shallow dish combine sugar and vinegar. Stir until sugar is completely dissolved. Marinate the pork chops in this for 15 to 20 minutes.

2. Heat the vegetable oil in a skillet. When it is hot add the pork chops and sauté over high heat for 4 minutes on each side, or until they caramelize.

3. Meanwhile, in a small skillet heat the walnut oil and sauté walnuts until golden brown.

4. Remove chops from the pan and deglaze pan with sherry. Reduce liquid over high heat to about 1 tablespoon.

5. Reduce the heat and add the walnuts, with their oil, and raisins. Return the chops to the pan and simmer 3 to 5 minutes, or until done.

6. Put the pork chops on individual plates and spoon sauce over them.

Wild Rice

SERVES 4

> 2 cups water
> 1 cup wild rice
> 4 tablespoons (1/2 stick) unsalted
>   butter, melted
> Fresh thyme to taste
> Salt and pepper to taste

1. In a pan, combine the water and rice. Bring to a boil, reduce heat, and simmer until rice reaches desired tenderness, 35 to 40 minutes. Drain well.

2. Add butter, thyme, and salt and pepper to taste and toss. Serve immediately.

Salad of Endive and Red Onion

SERVES 4

> 2 medium-size heads endive
> 1/2 red onion
> 1/2 cup any vinaigrette

1. Separate the leaves of endive or slice the endive diagonally into thin strips. Peel the red onion and chop coarsely.

2. Put the endive and onion in a salad bowl and toss well with the vinaigrette.

Fresh Pineapple and Coconut Curls

SERVES 4

> 1 coconut
> 1 pineapple

1. Pierce the eye of the coconut with a sharp knife. Shake out all the milk into a bowl and reserve.

2. Preheat the oven to 400°. Put the coconut in the oven and bake for 20 minutes. The coconut should crack or become easier to crack open with a hammer.

3. Cut the pineapple lengthwise in half, then cut each half into 4 wedges. Leaves should remain attached to the wedges.

4. First cut the core from the pineapple wedges and carefully slice the fruit from the skin, lengthwise, then crosswise. Arrange the pineapple wedges on a serving platter.

5. Using a sharp vegetable peeler, make ribbons of coconut and arrange them on top of the pineapple wedges. Sprinkle each with a tablespoon of coconut milk.

In France curly chicory is called frisée. In late winter and early spring the French often make an unusual salad of cold chicory greens, a warm poached egg, and a warm dressing. It is best served in large shallow soup plates (opposite) or deeper earthenware bowls.

Roast Leg of Lamb with Pan-Roasted Vegetables

*R*OAST LEG OF LAMB IS ONE of those dishes often overlooked by quick cooks. Pan-roasting meats and vegetables is a wonderfully easy way to cook, and results can be magnificent. Choose a roast that will fit comfortably in the pan with the vegetables, and make sure the oven is preheated. With lamb I like to add whole heads of garlic (they are delicious when roasted in this fashion), quartered potatoes, quartered baby artichokes, and possibly some peeled carrots and turnips. There must be good-quality olive oil in the pan to add flavor and help keep the vegetables from sticking during roasting.

Large sprigs of fresh rosemary and a few extra cloves of garlic are added for fragrance and flavor during roasting, and more rosemary is placed on the lamb before serving as a garnish.

MENU
Frisée Salad with Poached Egg and Lardons
Roast Leg of Lamb
Pan-Roasted Vegetables
French Bread
Dried Fruit Compote

Roast Leg of Lamb with Pan-Roasted Vegetables

SERVES 4 TO 6

1 small (4- to 5-pound) leg of lamb (or the shank end half of a large leg of lamb)

6 cloves garlic, peeled and sliced

1/2 cup olive oil
Salt and pepper to taste

4 to 6 sprigs fresh rosemary, or 2 tablespoons dried

4 to 6 roasting potatoes, washed and cut into quarters or eighths

6 small artichokes, quartered

6 to 8 whole heads of garlic
Optional or additional vegetables: baby turnips, leeks, shallots, carrots, parsnips

1 teaspoon salt
Fresh sprigs of rosemary (garnish)

1. Preheat the oven to 400°.

2. With the point of a small knife, make six small incisions at equal intervals under the skin of the lamb. Insert the garlic slices in these slits.

3. Rub the lamb with some of the oil and sprinkle with salt and pepper. Insert rosemary sprigs in the slits, or sprinkle the lamb with dried rosemary.

4. Pour the remaining oil into a shallow heavy baking dish or roaster and put lamb in it. Arrange vegetables around it and coat them with olive oil, 1 teaspoon salt, and pepper.

5. Roast lamb for 50 minutes to 1 hour, basting from time to time with the cooking juices.

6. Remove lamb from the oven and let it sit for about 10 minutes before carving. Keep the vegetables warm until ready to serve.

7. Arrange the lamb on a tray with the vegetables and garnish with sprigs of rosemary.

Frisée Salad with Poached Egg and Lardons

SERVES 6

6 fresh medium-size eggs
Allow a large handful of curly
chicory per serving

WARM VINAIGRETTE (Makes 2 cups)

3/4 cup thick bacon, cut into 3/4-
inch squares
1/2 cup red wine vinegar
1 cup olive oil
Salt and pepper to taste

1. Fill a shallow pan with water and bring to a boil. Reduce heat to simmer, add eggs one at a time, and poach until whites are set, about 3 minutes. (For well-shaped free-form poached eggs, use a spoon to contain the whites around the yolks while they cook.) Drain eggs on a plate lined with paper towel. Keep warm until ready to serve.

2. Arrange lettuce on individual plates and put a poached egg on top of each.

3. In a skillet cook the bacon until crispy. Pour off half the fat and add vinegar. Bring to a boil. Remove from the heat and whisk in the olive oil. Season with salt and pepper and pour immediately over the chicory.

Dried Fruit Compote

I love to make dried fruit compotes, and the combinations of fruits are endless. Look for good-quality dried fruits. Most health-food stores offer a large variety, as do some supermarkets. Allow 4 to 8 pieces of fruit per person. I always make a larger amount than necessary, for leftover compote is delicious the next day for breakfast.

Choose from dried figs, peaches, pears, apples, apricots, prunes, and raisins; let the fruits soak in water to cover for 1/2 hour. Cook the fruits in the water over a low flame until just tender. Add a cinnamon stick or two, some lemon zest, and a bit of sugar to the pot while cooking. Serve the fruits either warm or cold, with or without heavy cream. Offer a tablespoon of Cognac or Benedictine if you like.

Individual Pizzas

*T*HE PIZZA HAS MADE A BIG HIT all over America. In New York pizza parlors vie with one another for the most sausage, pepperoni, cheese, or mushrooms they can fit onto one crust; in Chicago the thick-crust pizza reigns supreme; and West Coast restaurants serve pizzas with exotic toppings of goat cheese, crab meat, and lobster. Of course, we all have our favorite type of pizza, and it is a great deal of fun—and easy—to bake the pizzas we love at home.

Our 1805 farmhouse was built with two kitchens—a summer kitchen, which was attached to the back of the house, and a winter kitchen, which had a large stone-and-brick cooking fireplace next to a large beehive baking oven that we discovered is perfect for making pizza. For years Andy and I had vowed to bake in the oven, but only recently did we really begin using it, with great success. The heat the oven contains, once enough hot coals are transferred to it from the main fire, is great enough to bake all day long. The floor of the oven is a type of soapstone, and the vaulted roof is made from brick. A wooden door shuts tight to hold in the heat. The flue lets smoke rise up through the main chimney.

Pizzas, of course, can be baked with almost equal success on baking sheets right in any home oven. Pizza dough can be made early in the day and left to rise, or it can be made ahead of time and frozen in uncooked individual-size crusts. The toppings can be set out in bowls and the pizzas created by whoever is going to consume them. One or two 8-inch pizzas are generally sufficient for one person.

We start the pizza meal off with a salad made with avocados and an unusual, but delicious, warm tomato-basil vinaigrette. Dessert should be something light, like orange ice cream or sherbet spooned into glasses and topped with a purée of black raspberries. A bit of Grand Marnier could be used as a topping for the ice cream if you have no berries.

Individual pizzas topped with black olives, tomatoes, capers, prosciutto, mushrooms, and cheeses are baked in the beehive oven of our kitchen. The long-handled wooden pizza paddles I use, called "peels," can be purchased in restaurant supply houses.

❧

MENU
Individual Pizzas
Avocado with Warm Tomato and Basil Vinaigrette
Orange Ice Cream with Black Raspberry Sauce

Individual Pizzas

MAKES 4 INDIVIDUAL PIZZAS

SUGGESTED TOPPINGS, PER PIZZA

6 black olives (Sicilian type, pitted), 1/2 cup stewed plum tomatoes, 1 tablespoon capers, 1/2 cup grated mozzarella cheese

1/4 cup cooked peas, 8 strips prosciutto, 1/2 cup ricotta cheese, 1/2 cup grated mozzarella cheese

1/2 cup stewed tomatoes, 6 anchovy fillets, 4 sprigs fresh thyme, 1/4 cup Fontina cheese, 1/4 cup mozzarella cheese

1/2 cup goat cheese, 1 tablespoon fresh rosemary, 2 tablespoons olive oil, 3 strips cooked bacon, 1/2 cup sautéed mushrooms, 1/2 cup mozzarella cheese

DOUGH

1 package active dry yeast or 1/3 cake fresh yeast
1 1/4 cups lukewarm water
3 cups unbleached flour
1 1/2 teaspoons salt
1 tablespoon olive oil

1. In a large mixing bowl dissolve the yeast in 1/2 cup lukewarm water. Let it proof for 10 minutes.

2. Add the flour, salt, olive oil, and remaining water. Mix well and knead until the dough is smooth, about 10 minutes. This can be done by hand or with an electric mixer with a dough hook. Add more flour if necessary to make a smooth, silky dough.

3. Put the dough in an oiled bowl, cover with a cloth, and set aside in a warm place until it doubles in bulk. This should take 1 hour or longer. Punch down the dough and let it rest for another 10 minutes.

4. Divide the dough into 4 pieces and roll each piece into a flat circle approximately 10 inches in diameter. At this point you can use the dough immediately or freeze it, well wrapped, for future use. (Frozen crusts must be thoroughly thawed before being used.)

5. Preheat oven to 450°. Brush the tops of the circles of dough with olive oil.

6. Arrange ingredients evenly over the dough. The top layer should be mozzarella or Fontina cheese.

7. Put on a baking sheet that has been dusted with cornmeal and bake until pizza is brown around the edges and the topping has cooked and the cheese has melted, about 15 minutes. (If pizza seems to be getting too dark, reduce oven heat to 425°.)

Avocado with Warm Tomato
and Basil Vinaigrette

SERVES 4

TOMATO AND BASIL VINAIGRETTE
(Makes 1 cup)

2 *large ripe tomatoes, peeled,*
   seeded, and diced
1/2 *cup chopped basil leaves*
4 *tablespoons red wine vinegar*
1/2 *cup light olive oil*
2 *tablespoons Dijon mustard*
   Salt and pepper to taste

2 *avocados, halved and pitted*

1. In a saucepan combine all vinaigrette ingredients. Bring to a simmer.

2. Put the avocado halves on individual plates. Spoon the warm dressing over the avocados, garnish each with a basil leaf, and serve immediately.

Orange Ice Cream with Black Raspberry Sauce

SERVES 4

Serve scoops of orange ice cream (or sherbet) with a black raspberry or blackberry sauce. To make the sauce, press 1 pint fresh berries or one 10-ounce package thawed frozen berries through a fine sieve. Add sugar to taste and a tablespoon of blackberry liqueur, crème de cassis, or Grand Marnier.

Saffron-Broiled Chicken Quarters

*L*ATE SPRING IS A TIME FOR first peas, garden asparagus, sour cherries, baby lettuce, crispy radishes, and tender onions and leeks. I love to use these early offerings from the garden in my family's meals, and find that I rarely have to shop during this time of year, other than making occasional trips to the butcher or fishmonger.

The fresh pea soup in this menu is simple and delicious. I serve it throughout the summer, later substituting frozen tiny peas for fresh garden peas. I often offer it cold, with a spoonful of crème fraîche and a fresh mint leaf as garnish.

The broiled chicken is one of my family's favorite chicken recipes. Nothing could be simpler than broiled chicken, but the sprinkling of saffron and subtle taste of lemon make this very special. The fennel salad is an unusual combination of the fennel bulb (a slightly licorice-tasting vegetable), red onions, and *pumate,* sun-dried Italian tomatoes preserved in olive oil, which can be found in gourmet shops.

A spring meal that begins with fresh pea soup looks charming presented in Quimperware bowls and plates. A yellowware "basket" (opposite), the only one I've seen, is the vase for a small bouquet of early parrot tulips.

❧

MENU
Fresh Pea Soup with Croutons
Saffron-Broiled Chicken Quarters
Fennel Salad with Red Onion
and Sun-Dried Tomatoes
Baked Bananas with Rum and Butter

Fresh Pea Soup with Croutons

SERVES 4

3 tablespoons unsalted butter
2 cups fresh or frozen peas
1 medium-size head butter lettuce, chopped
4 scallions, chopped
6 cups chicken stock or water
Salt and pepper to taste
6 leaves fresh tarragon, finely chopped
Croutons *
Heavy cream or crème fraîche (optional)

1. Melt butter in a pot and add peas, lettuce, and scallions. Cook over medium-low heat for 5 minutes. Do not brown them.

2. Add stock, bring to a boil, reduce to a simmer, and cook until peas are tender, 10 to 15 minutes.

3. Purée the soup in a blender or food processor. Season with salt and pepper and add tarragon. Serve hot or cold with croutons. You can enrich the soup with a few tablespoons of heavy cream or crème fraîche, if you wish.

    * To make croutons, sauté 1/2-inch cubes of French bread in olive oil until brown and crispy.

Saffron-Broiled Chicken Quarters

SERVES 4

2 small broiling chickens, quartered with backs removed
Salt and pepper to taste
1/4 teaspoon saffron
Juice of 1 lemon

1. Preheat the broiler. Put chicken pieces, skin side down, on a foil-covered baking sheet (this makes clean-up easier).

2. Sprinkle lightly with salt and pepper, half the saffron, and half the lemon juice. Broil for 8 to 10 minutes, until crispy and golden brown.

3. Turn chicken pieces and season with salt and pepper and remaining saffron and lemon juice. Broil for another 8 to 10 minutes, adjusting the heat if necessary so the skin turns crispy and golden. Serve hot or warm.

Fennel Salad with Red Onion and Sun-Dried Tomatoes

SERVES 4

2 large bulbs fennel
1 medium-size red onion, peeled and coarsely chopped
6 sun-dried tomatoes, cut into thin strips
1/4 cup Italian parsley (leaves only)

VINAIGRETTE (Makes 3/4 cup)

1 tablespoon oil from sun-dried tomatoes
6 tablespoons olive oil
3 tablespoons tarragon vinegar
Salt and pepper to taste

1. Trim the fennel, removing any hard core and stalk. Cut into thin strips lengthwise.

2. Combine fennel, onion, tomatoes, and parsley in a serving bowl.

3. In a small mixing bowl combine all the dressing ingredients and pour over the salad. Toss well and serve.

Note: This salad will retain its crispness and flavor for several hours.

Baked Bananas with Rum and Butter

SERVES 4

4 tablespoons (1/2 stick) unsalted butter
4 medium bananas, peeled and halved lengthwise
1/4 cup brown sugar
1/4 cup dark rum

1. Preheat oven to 400°.

2. Butter a glass baking dish large enough to hold all the bananas in one layer.

3. Put the bananas, cut side down, in the dish. Sprinkle with sugar and rum, and dot with the remaining butter. Bake until sugar is melted and bananas are tender but not mushy, about 10 minutes. Serve hot.

Assorted Wursts and Mustards

Sausages cook on the range of the Stamford, Connecticut, cast-iron stove Andy and I installed in the living room of our new barn. I found the stove, rusty and pitted, at a tag sale and drove it to Vermont, where it was refurbished. It now functions both as a cooker and a heater in the barn. My cast-iron pots, pans, skillets, and muffin tins are carefully seasoned and used exclusively on the wood-burning ranges of the barn. Also displayed is part of my collection of antique strainers and copper molds and Andy's collection of pinkware bowls.

❦

MENU
Early Spring Salad
Assorted Wursts and Mustards
Sauerkraut with Apples
Bran Rolls and Rye Bread

I'VE ALWAYS LIKED SAUSAGES.
My very favorite when I was growing up was Kurowycky's kielbasa, which
we had every Easter and Christmas. Nowadays, on one of those chilly early
spring evenings, I like to stoke up one of my cast-iron cookstoves, get down
all the cast-iron skillets, and cook up a feast of sausages: wiesswursts, brat-
wursts, knackwursts, bauernwursts, and kielbasas.

Sausages can be poached in large skillets, as directed in the recipe that
follows, or cooked directly on a charcoal or gas-fired grill. I tend to prefer
German sausages cooked in skillets and Italian or Spanish sausages grilled
over the coals.

I have a cast-iron pan that is divided into six sections—for corn bread,
I suppose—which I use for mustards. Another skillet is filled with sauerkraut and apples. Homemade or store-bought bran rolls and sliced rye bread
are heaped up to accompany the sausages.

For a salad try early spring greens—dandelion, chicory, spinach, escarole, and small leaves of Swiss chard—in a warm balsamic vinegar dressing.

For dessert make or purchase a spice cake, and serve it with softly
whipped cream.

❦

Early Spring Salad
SERVES 4

*Allow about a handful of any
combination of dandelion,
chicory, spinach, escarole, or
small leaves of Swiss chard per
person*

BALSAMIC VINEGAR DRESSING
(Makes 1 cup)

1/3 cup balsamic vinegar
  2 tablespoons Dijon mustard
3/4 cup Italian olive oil
1/2 teaspoon salt
     Freshly ground black pepper

1. Arrange the salad greens in a bowl.

2. Warm the vinegar over low heat in a small saucepan.

3. In a large mixing bowl combine the warm vinegar and mustard. Slowly
whisk in the olive oil until the mixture becomes thick and creamy. Season
with salt and pepper. Pour the dressing over the greens, toss well, and serve
immediately.

Assorted Wursts and Mustards

SERVES 4

**Allowing 2 to 3 per person,
choose an assortment of the
following sausages: weiswurst
(uncooked veal and pork
sausage), bratwurst (uncooked
pork sausage), knackwurst
(cooked pork and beef
sausage), kielbasa (uncooked
smoked Polish sausage),
bauernwurst (cooked beef and
pork sausage)**
2 cups white wine or water
**4 tablespoons (1/2 stick) unsalted
butter**
Assorted mustards

1. Pierce the skin of the sausages in several places to prevent them from
bursting while cooking. In a skillet poach the sausages in wine for 20 minutes. Remove the sausages and discard the liquid.*

2. Melt butter in the skillet and brown sausages on all sides over medium
heat. Serve with an assortment of mustards.

* You can add the cooking liquid to the sauerkraut and apples (see
recipe that follows) as a substitute for the wine called for in that recipe.

Sauerkraut with Apples

SERVES 4

1 pound sauerkraut
6 small white onions
2 medium Red Delicious apples
Juice of 1/2 lemon
2 cups white wine
Salt and pepper to taste

1. Put the sauerkraut in a sieve or colander, rinse thoroughly with cold
water, and drain, squeezing out as much moisture as possible.

2. Peel the onions, leaving them whole, and cut an X in the bottom of
each. Wash, core, and slice the apples and put in a bowl. Squeeze lemon
juice over the apples to keep them from turning brown. Set aside.

3. Put the sauerkraut, onions, and wine in a large saucepan and cook over
medium heat for 15 minutes.

4. Add the apple slices and cook another 10 minutes, or until they are
tender. Season with salt and pepper.

Seafood Salad

*T*HIS SEAFOOD SALAD IS THE creation of my friend and fellow worker Jane Stacey. When I asked her why she liked it so much, she answered that it was fast to prepare, it offered a lot of variety, and each portion could be arranged on individual plates and refrigerated until ready to serve. She later admitted that it was really the chance to arrange artistically the colorful ingredients that most appealed to her. As you can see in the photograph, Jane's style of arranging is casual yet purposeful. With each spoonful one would get a bit of everything in the salad.

The accompanying dish—ravioli with mushrooms and sugar snap peas —is served hot, and again is chosen for its fast, easy preparation as well as for the fact that it is satisfying and delicious. Fresh ravioli with fillings of meat, cheese, or seafood are now available in many stores. Ravioli can also be homemade (in which case they should be made when one has time, and frozen), and Jane suggests fillings of wild mushrooms, lobster, or crab meat. Sugar snap peas are a new and pleasing alternative to snow peas—they are a bit sweeter and their flavor is more like that of tiny fresh spring peas. They are very easy to grow, and every spring garden should have a row.

A clear glass casserole dish shows off the colors and textures of this light seafood salad to its best advantage. An oval copper **poêle**, *or chef's skillet, holds the ravioli.*

❧

MENU
Seafood Salad
Ravioli with Mushrooms and Sugar Snap Peas
Strawberries with Cassis Syrup

Seafood Salad

SERVES 6

12 large shrimp, peeled
12 mussels
12 to 14 clams
1 pound bay scallops
1/2 cup dry white wine
2 red bell peppers (or one red and one yellow) or any sweet pepper, roasted *
1 Italian frying pepper
2 tablespoons olive oil
8 to 10 Greek olives
5 small Japanese radishes, peeled and sliced lengthwise
2 whole scallions, julienned
2 tablespoons chopped flat parsley

VINAIGRETTE (Makes 1 cup)

1/4 cup red wine vinegar
2 tablespoons olive oil
3/4 cup vegetable oil
1 clove garlic, peeled and minced
1 tablespoon Dijon mustard
Salt and pepper to taste

1. Steam the shrimp until pink, about 2 minutes. Do not overcook. Set aside.

2. Steam the mussels and clams until they open, removing them as they open, about 3 minutes. Do not overcook or they will shrink.

3. Poach the scallops in the white wine for 1 minute. Drain.

4. Arrange the shrimp, mussels, clams, and scallops on a serving plate.

5. Core peppers and cut into quarters or sixths. Heat the oil in a frying pan and fry all the peppers for 1 or 2 minutes. Arrange them on the platter with the seafood. Add olives and radish slices.

6. In a mixing bowl combine all the ingredients for the vinaigrette. Whisk well and pour over the seafood salad. Sprinkle the scallions and parsley over the top of the salad.

 * To roast the peppers, put them directly on the gas burner over high heat or under the broiler until the skin turns black, turning them frequently to roast all sides. Put them in a paper bag and close it. Let peppers sweat 4 to 5 minutes, then rub off skins. The broiler of an electric stove achieves the same results.

Ravioli with Mushrooms and Sugar Snap Peas

SERVES 6

1/4 pound whole sugar snap peas
1 pound meat ravioli, fresh or frozen
5 tablespoons unsalted butter
1 clove garlic, halved
1/4 pound small mushrooms
1/4 cup grated Parmesan cheese
Salt and pepper to taste

1. In a medium saucepan bring lightly salted water to boil and cook the peas, uncovered, for 2 minutes. Drain. Cool peas in ice water. Drain well.

2. Cook ravioli in a large kettle of boiling water until tender. Drain and set aside.

3. In a large skillet melt butter over medium-high heat. Sauté the garlic and brown the mushrooms slightly. Remove garlic.

4. Add ravioli and peas to skillet and toss well with cheese. Season to taste. Serve at once.

Strawberries with Cassis Syrup

SERVES 6

2 pints medium-size strawberries
1/4 cup crème de cassis
1 tablespoon sugar
1/2 cup water

1. Stem and wash the strawberries. Drain.

2. In a small saucepan combine crème de cassis, sugar, and water. Cook over medium heat until the mixture is reduced to about 1/2 cup. Chill.

3. Serve the strawberries in individual bowls and pour syrup over them.

A simple meal for two looks elegant when served on hand-painted Meissen china with antique English fish forks and knives. Pouilly-Fuissé white wine would complement the salmon perfectly. Very thin slices of Golden Delicious apple in a puff pastry shell (opposite) make a wonderful light dessert for this dinner.

Broiled Salmon Steaks

MENU
Broiled Salmon Steaks
Baby Peas and Butter Lettuce
Baked Rice
French Rolls
Paper-Thin Apple Tarts

only cuisine for which I have an incessant craving, is Japanese food. I have visited Japan several times with my husband and have had many memorable meals there. At one tiny Japanese inn, after a fantastic sashimi appetizer, we were served delicate salmon fillets grilled with salt, lime juice, and soy sauce. For this menu I use salmon steaks, cut from the center of a 6- or 7-pound Norwegian salmon. The flesh is fine, light pink, and exceedingly sweet. (I use the same Norwegian salmon, when I can find it, for gravlax and for salmon tartare, two dishes that call for extremely fresh fish.) The preheated broiler is the secret here—this way, the salmon cooks quickly and evenly and remains tender and moist.

For dessert, a square of puff pastry (buy frozen or make your own and freeze it), topped with the thinnest slices of apple and a sprinkling of sugar, is baked until light and golden in color. Make an extra tart or two if you have the pastry, for they are consumed with ease!

Broiled Salmon Steaks

SERVES 2

> *Juice of 1 lime*
> *2 teaspoons soy sauce*
> *2 center-cut salmon steaks, 1 1/4 inches thick*
> *Kosher salt to taste*

1. Preheat the broiler. In a bowl combine lime juice and soy sauce.

2. Put the salmon steaks on a baking sheet and baste with the lime-soy mixture and lightly sprinkle with salt. Broil 4 inches from the flame for about 5 minutes. Turn the salmon, brush with lime-soy mixture, sprinkle with salt, and cook 5 minutes more, or until fish is done. Serve at once.

Baby Peas and Butter Lettuce

SERVES 2

> *2 tablespoons (1/4 stick) unsalted butter*
> *1/2 pound baby peas, shelled (frozen petits pois can be substituted)*
> *Pinch of sugar*
> *1/4 cup water*
> *1 small head butter lettuce, cut into a fine chiffonade*
> *Salt and pepper to taste*

1. Melt the butter in a saucepan over medium heat. Add the peas, sugar, and water and cook just until tender, about 2 minutes.

2. Add the lettuce and toss over the heat until wilted. Season lightly with salt and pepper and serve.

Baked Rice

SERVES 2

2 cups chicken stock
2 tablespoons (1/4 stick) unsalted
   butter
1 shallot, finely minced
1 cup long-grain rice or Japanese
   rice
  Salt and freshly ground pepper
   to taste
  Sprigs of fresh thyme, parsley,
   chervil, dill, or summer savory
   (optional)

1. Preheat oven to 375°.

2. Bring chicken stock to a boil.

3. Melt the butter in a heavy casserole over medium-high heat. Add the shallot and cook until translucent, 3 to 4 minutes.

4. Reduce heat to medium, add rice, and cook until it turns opaque, about 5 minutes. Pour in the boiling stock, add herbs, if desired, cover, and put in the middle of the hot oven. Bake for 18 minutes. The liquid should be absorbed and the rice fluffy. Correct seasoning and serve at once.

Paper-Thin Apple Tarts

SERVES 4

1/4 pound puff pastry (homemade or
   store-bought)
2 Granny Smith apples
1 teaspoon sugar
1/4 cup apple jelly, melted (optional)

1. Roll the puff pastry into two 8-inch squares about 1/4 to 1/8 inch thick. Cut a 3/4-inch strip off each side. Brush the edge of the squares with water and "paste" the strips along each edge of the square to form a raised border. Chill thoroughly.

2. Preheat oven to 400°.

3. Peel and core the apples. Cut them in half and place halves on their flat sides. Slice apples into paper-thin slices across the core.

4. With a fork, prick the bottom of the tart shells every 1/2 inch. Do not prick edges. Arrange the apple slices in overlapping rows on the tart shells. Sprinkle with sugar and bake for 15 to 20 minutes, or until edges of pastry puff are brown and the sugar caramelizes.

5. To make the glaze, melt the apple jelly and brush it on top of the tarts after they have been removed from the oven. Serve warm.

Veal Scallopine alla Marsala

THIS IS A MORE FORMAL MENU for a spring dinner than the preceding menus. The menu is for four people, but because the preparation is quite simple, it could be expanded to serve eight or twelve, with additional cooking time, of course.

The first course of a large globe artichoke, one per person, served with lemon zest butter, is impressive. Serve the butter in small dishes next to each artichoke and provide a waste plate for the eaten leaves.

The veal recipe calls for the finest veal available. The scallops should be cut from the leg of veal, each piece just large enough for one serving. I prefer the veal to be cut extremely thin and then pounded slightly to even out the thickness, rather than cut a thicker slice and pound the life out of it. I find that the veal pieces done this way shrink less during the sautéing and retain more of the original shape and size. I try to buy white veal, marked "Plume de Veau" in our area. When preparing this type of veal, remember that it requires very little cooking time—4 to 6 minutes at the most.

The carrots are a tender and delicious accompaniment to the veal. The small amount of sugar added while the carrots cook sweetens even the more wintry varieties of carrots. If you try this recipe with tender baby carrots freshly picked from the garden, you can omit the sugar.

Add a tossed salad if you wish, although I think that with the artichoke the meal doesn't really need one.

For dessert, whip up a zabaglione using Grand Marnier, since Marsala, the traditional flavoring, is in the veal. It takes a few extra minutes at the stove to create this light and frothy concoction, but the results are certainly worth it.

Veal scallops, garnished with only a sprig of fresh thyme, look regal on an intricately patterned Haviland plate. A silk rag runner, in muted shades, is the covering for this table. An appropriate wine would be an Italian Pinot Chardonnay or Grigio.

MENU
Artichokes with Lemon Butter
Veal Scallopine alla Marsala
Carrots with Cream
Hot, Crusty Italian Bread
Zabaglione with Grand Marnier

Artichokes with Lemon Butter

SERVES 4

4 artichokes
4 shallots, minced
4 tablespoons olive oil
4 tablespoons chopped parsley
1 teaspoon salt
  Freshly ground pepper to taste
1 cup (2 sticks) unsalted butter
  Juice and zest of 2 lemons
2 sprigs fresh thyme

1. Cut off the artichoke stems and 1 inch of the top with a sharp knife. Using scissors, cut off the prickly points of the leaves.

2. Stand artichokes upright in a deep pot just large enough to hold them. Sprinkle with shallots, oil, parsley, salt, and pepper. Add enough water to reach a third of the way up the artichokes. Cover.

3. Bring the water to a boil. Reduce to simmer and cook for 20 to 30 minutes, until artichokes are tender but not mushy. Remove them from the pan and set aside.

4. Put the butter, lemon juice, and thyme in a saucepan. Melt the butter over medium-low heat. Remove the thyme sprigs, add the lemon zest, and serve the butter in individual bowls with warm artichokes.

Veal Scallopine alla Marsala

SERVES 4

4 tablespoons (1/2 stick) unsalted
  butter
4 tablespoons olive oil
1 to 1 1/4 pounds veal scallops
  Juice of one lemon
3/4 cup Marsala wine
  Salt and freshly ground pepper
  Sprigs of fresh thyme

1. Very lightly coat each scallop with flour.

2. In a large skillet heat butter with oil until very hot but not smoking. Quickly brown veal on both sides.

3. Lower heat to medium and add lemon juice and Marsala. Simmer veal another 4 to 5 minutes. Sprinkle with salt and pepper. Serve immediately, garnished with fresh thyme sprigs.

Carrots with Cream

SERVES 4

> 1 pound carrots, peeled and cut
>   into 1/4-inch rounds
> 3 tablespoons unsalted butter
> 1/4 teaspoon salt
> 1/2 teaspoon sugar
> 1 1/2 cups water
> 1/2 cup heavy cream
> 1 tablespoon chopped parsley or
>   chervil

1. Put the carrots, butter, salt, sugar, and water in a saucepan. Cook, uncovered, over medium heat until carrots are tender and water has almost evaporated, about 15 minutes.

2. Stir in cream and parsley. Cook gently for about 2 minutes more, until cream is warm. Serve hot.

Zabaglione with Grand Marnier

SERVES 4

> 6 egg yolks
> 2 tablespoons sugar
> 1/4 cup Sauterne or champagne
> 1 tablespoon orange zest
> 3 tablespoons Grand Marnier
> 1 cup heavy cream, whipped
>   (optional)

1. Beat the egg yolks and sugar in a double boiler over simmering water until thick and pale yellow.

2. Add the wine and orange zest and continue cooking, whisking vigorously, until mixture thickens enough to coat the back of a spoon. Stir in the Grand Marnier.

3. Serve warm or chilled over fruit or pour into dessert glasses and serve with whipped cream. Or chill the zabaglione, fold in whipped cream, and serve in dessert glasses.

Summer

✣

. . . .

Spicy Lobster with Linguine

WE LIVE VERY CLOSE TO THE shores of Long Island Sound, where the waters abound with mussels, little-neck and cherrystone clams, and lobsters. We eat lobsters many times during the course of the summer and are always trying new recipes using these delicious crustaceans. Lisa Krieger, one of my assistants, made this spicy lobster with linguine one hot summer day, and I've made it many times since.

I use 1 1/4 pound lobsters and steam them for 8 to 10 minutes over rapidly boiling water to which dry white wine, vermouth, or vodka has been added. The lobsters are split while still hot, and the chopped tails and claws (we eat the bodies another time) are added to hot linguine that has been tossed with a spicy red pepper–tomato sauce. Use fresh garden-ripe plum tomatoes or good-quality canned tomatoes for the sauce. Serve the pasta with sautéed sugar snap peas and lots of French bread and sweet butter.

The dessert is a wonderful combination of greengage plums baked with Sauterne and served with heavy cream. Greengage plums are available for only a month or so during the latter part of the summer; other baking varieties will do, like Santa Rosa, Golden Shiro, or Mount Royal.

Summertime gives us the opportunity to expand our dining out of the confines of our homes into areas more spacious, varied, and inspired. We are tempted to try more unusual menus, too, such as this spicy pasta dish served in a shallow stoneware pie plate.

✣

MENU
Melon with Prosciutto
Spicy Lobster with Linguine
Sautéed Sugar Snap Peas
French Bread and Sweet Butter
Baked Whole Green Plums

Melon with Prosciutto

SERVES 6

1 large cantaloupe, honeydew, or
   Persian melon
12 thin slices prosciutto
   Wedges of lime or lemon

1. Cut the melon in half and remove the seeds. Cut each half into thirds; each of these will be one serving. Cut each wedge into 3 pieces. Peel them with a sharp knife and put on individual serving plates. (I often use two types of melons, or wedges of papaya or mango, or any combination, alternating the colors on each plate.)

2. Drape 2 slices of prosciutto over each plate of melon wedges and serve with wedges of lemon or lime. Do not let the dish get warm or the ham will be oily and the melon mushy.

Note: Six quartered ripe figs or 3 sliced papayas or mangoes are also wonderful with prosciutto. Be sure to buy good-quality prosciutto that is tender and dark red. Try to get center-cut slices, which generally are larger and better-textured. Black Forest ham is a good substitute if prosciutto is not available.

Spicy Lobster with Linguine

SERVES 6

1 1/2 cups white wine (or vermouth or
      vodka)
   6 lobsters
   4 tablespoons olive oil
   3 cloves garlic, minced
      Hot pepper flakes to taste
   2 28-ounce cans imported
      tomatoes
1/4 cup fresh mint leaves, chopped
1 1/2 pounds linguine
      Salt and pepper to taste

1. Combine approximately 1 cup water with the wine in a large pot and steam the lobsters for 8 to 10 minutes. Cool. Split the lobsters and cut the tails and claws of each into 6 pieces; reserve the bodies for other uses.

2. Heat olive oil in a large saucepan over medium heat. Add garlic and sauté for 2 minutes. Add hot pepper flakes.

3. Chop the tomatoes and add them to the saucepan along with the mint leaves. Simmer over low heat for 3 minutes. Set aside in a warm place.

4. Cook the pasta in a large pot of salted boiling water until *al dente.* Drain. Put linguine on a serving platter and arrange lobster on top. Pour sauce over, toss, season, and serve.

Sautéed Sugar Snap Peas

SERVES 6

> 4 to 5 tablespoons unsalted butter
> 1 1/2 pounds sugar snap peas, strings removed
> 1/2 teaspoon sugar
> Salt and pepper to taste

1. Melt the butter in a large skillet and sauté the peas until tender, 3 to 4 minutes.

2. Sprinkle with sugar and toss well. Season with salt and pepper and serve.

Baked Whole Green Plums

SERVES 6

> 2 tablespoons (1/4 stick) unsalted butter
> 1/2 cup sugar
> 6 large greengage plums or 12 small plums
> 1/2 cup Sauterne
> 1 cup heavy cream

1. Preheat oven to 350°. Butter a baking dish that is just large enough to hold the plums. Sprinkle half of the sugar over the bottom of the dish. Arrange the plums in the dish, stem side down.

2. Sprinkle on remaining sugar and dot plums with butter. Bake for 5 minutes and add the Sauterne. Continue baking until plums are soft but not mushy or split, 20 to 25 minutes. (If they start to split, reduce the oven heat.)

3. Remove from the oven, allow them to cool for 5 minutes, and serve warm with heavy cream.

Grilled Butterflied Squabs
with Mustard Sauce

I HADN'T COOKED MANY SQUABS before last fall, when I was commissioned by a client to prepare 568 of these small game birds (actually pigeons) for a formal sit-down dinner. My assistants and I tried several recipes before settling on one for roasted squab with a wild rice, bread, and fruit stuffing. The squabs were stuffed, trussed, and browned in butter before being roasted quickly in a hot oven. Never again will I serve squabs to so large a group, for many of the guests did not enjoy picking at the small, bony birds, and some balked at the idea of eating a pigeon the traditional way, just slightly pink. I think that the following recipe is much more successful. When squabs are marinated and grilled, the skin is nicely browned, the flesh very flavorful, and the meat tender. Fresh corn on the cob, roasted over the same coals, is extremely tasty when brushed with cayenne-lime butter and cooked until brown.

The salad is a simple concoction of fresh mozzarella cheese (the packaged variety is an acceptable, though not as interesting, alternative) and red, ripe tomatoes, simply flavored with green olive oil and basil.

This is a menu to use over and over again. If squabs are unavailable, try split quails or partridges. Pheasants, too, would be wonderful cooked this way. For less adventuresome palates, or for those who can't obtain game birds, try Cornish hens or even small broiler chickens.

An old cutting board made of one wide piece of yellow pine displays the grilled butterflied squabs, roasted corn, and salad of fresh summer tomatoes, mozzarella cheese, and small-leaf basil.

❊

MENU
Grilled Butterflied Squabs with Mustard Sauce
Roasted Corn on the Cob
Sliced Tomatoes with Mozzarella and Basil
Strawberries and Melon Balls in Bourbon

Grilled Butterflied Squabs with Mustard Sauce

SERVES 6

> 6 squabs
> 1/4 cup olive oil
> 1/2 cup vegetable oil
> 1/2 cup Dijon mustard
> 1/4 cup whole-grain mustard
>   (Moutarde de Meaux)
> 1/4 cup honey
> 3 tablespoons champagne or white
>   wine vinegar

1. Split the squabs in half.

2. In a large bowl combine all the remaining ingredients and marinate the squabs in this mixture for several hours or overnight, turning them occasionally.

3. To cook the squabs, grill them 6 inches above hot coals for 10 to 12 minutes on each side. The squabs should be nicely browned.

Note: If you use a broiler, put the squabs 4 to 5 inches under the preheated broiler skin side down, and cook for 8 to 10 minutes. Turn the squabs and continue broiling until the skin is crispy and brown. Adjust the heat during broiling to prevent burning. I like to serve the squabs with the meat slightly pink, but cook to suit your taste.

Roasted Corn on the Cob

SERVES 6

> Juice of 2 limes
> Large pinch cayenne pepper
> 8 tablespoons (1 stick) unsalted
>   butter, melted
> 12 ears fresh, tender young corn,
>   husked
> Coarse salt to taste

1. Mix the lime juice, cayenne pepper, and melted butter in a small mixing bowl.

2. Roast the corn over the coals, brushing often with the melted butter mixture. Roast until the kernels are soft and golden brown, turning often, about 10 minutes. Serve immediately with extra butter and salt.

Sliced Tomatoes with Mozzarella and Basil

SERVES 6

6 large, very ripe tomatoes, cut into 1/3-inch slices
1 pound fresh mozzarella, cut in 1/3-inch slices
6 sprigs basil (small-leaf variety preferable)
4 tablespoons green olive oil
Coarse salt and pepper to taste

1. Arrange alternating slices of tomatoes and mozzarella on a platter.

2. Place basil on top of the tomatoes and mozzarella. Sprinkle with olive oil and season with salt and pepper.

Note: Finely chopped sun-dried tomatoes (*pumate*) are wonderful sprinkled on top of the tomatoes.

Strawberries and Melon Balls in Bourbon

SERVES 6

1 large melon, seeded
1 quart ripe, red strawberries
1/2 cup bourbon
1/3 cup sugar, or to taste
Sprigs of fresh mint

1. Cut the melon pulp into small balls with a melon baller.

2. Hull the berries and arrange in a bowl with the melon balls. Pour on the bourbon, sprinkle with sugar, stir, and set aside until ready to serve. (Refrigerate if you will not be serving within an hour.)

3. Spoon fruit onto serving plates or into goblets and decorate with mint.

Tortellini with Butter and Parmesan Cheese

THE KITCHEN IN OUR NEW BARN boasts two beautiful green enamel stoves. The stoves inspired me to begin a collection of green kitchen things. It is amazing how extensive "kitchen green" was in the twenties, thirties, and forties, in both the United States and England. It is almost impossible to find anything modern colored that particular shade; I think the reaction against its prevalence made it almost extinct. Nevertheless, it is interesting, and Andy and I have designed a whole room around that color.

This menu was inspired by Signora Adorni, the housekeeper-cook of a lovely villa in Camaiore, Italy. It was she who showed me how to pound and chop pesto by hand, how to cut pasta for tortellini, and how to prepare the most delectable of soups from ripe, plump tomatoes. Each year Andy and I grow many varieties of tomatoes, and this soup recipe makes good use of them.

The carpaccio, with a parsley-caper-anchovy-cornichon sauce, makes a colorful first course. Use the leanest prime top round you can get; make sure all the fat is removed and the slices are cut almost paper-thin.

I often use store-bought tortellini with fillings of chicken, veal, or spinach. If I have time, I make my own, with more unusual fillings like pumpkin, lobster, or cheese. My friend Inez Norwich makes extraordinary pasta for tortellini. Her secret ingredient for extra-tender dough: the yolks from quail eggs.

Signora Adorni used to pick the juiciest, most perfect peaches and plums from her trees and serve them with her own fresh lime juice. This makes a wonderfully refreshing ending to the meal.

Depression-era pottery bowls sitting on the stove hold the tortellini and the garden-fresh tomato soup. The first course of carpaccio (paper-thin slices of the freshest lean beef), with a pungent caper-parsley sauce, looks colorful and appealing on green pottery plates.

❦

MENU
Carpaccio with Caper-Parsley Sauce
Tuscan Tomato Soup
Tortellini with Butter and Parmesan Cheese
Plums and Peaches in Lime Juice

Carpaccio with Caper-Parsley Sauce

SERVES 6

1/2 pound beef top round, all fat removed

CAPER-PARSLEY SAUCE
(Makes 1 cup)

3 tablespoons white vinegar
6 cornichons
1 cup chopped parsley
2 cloves garlic, peeled
2 anchovy fillets
3 tablespoons tiny capers
1 tablespoon chopped onion
1 tablespoon Dijon mustard
2/3 cup olive oil

1. Cut the beef into paper-thin slices. Arrange 2 slices of meat on each serving plate. Chill until ready to serve.

2. In a food processor or blender purée the vinegar, cornichons, parsley, garlic, anchovies, capers, onion, and mustard. Add the oil a drop at a time while the machine is running, to make a thick green sauce. Chill until ready to serve.

3. To serve, spoon several tablespoons of sauce on the meat.

Tortellini with Butter and Parmesan Cheese

SERVES 6

2 tablespoons olive oil
1 1/2 pounds tortellini
1 cup grated Parmesan cheese
1/4 pound (1 stick) unsalted butter, melted
Salt and pepper to taste
1/4 cup chopped fresh basil

1. In a large pot bring lightly salted water to a boil. Add olive oil and the tortellini. Cook just until the tortellini begin to float to the surface. Drain well in a colander.

2. Put tortellini in a serving bowl and toss with Parmesan cheese and hot melted butter. Season with salt and pepper. Sprinkle with chopped basil.

Tuscan Tomato Soup

SERVES 6

2 tablespoons (1/4 stick) unsalted butter
1/4 cup olive oil
2 carrots, peeled and finely minced
2 stalks celery, finely minced
2 onions, finely minced
10 large ripe tomatoes, skinned and seeded, or 2 quarts canned tomatoes
Pinch of sugar
1/2 cup chopped fresh basil leaves
Salt and pepper to taste
Freshly grated Parmesan cheese (optional)

1. Heat butter and oil in a large heavy pot. Cook the carrots, celery, and onion over medium-low heat for 20 minutes, or until soft. Do not brown them.

2. Add the tomatoes, sugar, and half the basil to the pot and cook 15 to 20 minutes.

3. Stir in the remaining basil, season with salt and pepper, and serve immediately. Sprinkle with Parmesan cheese, if desired.

Plums and Peaches in Lime Juice

SERVES 6

3 freestone peaches
6 freestone plums
Juice of 2 or 3 limes
Freshly grated nutmeg to taste (optional)

1. In a large pot bring water to a boil and add the peaches and plums; simmer for 15 to 30 seconds. Remove fruit from the water with a slotted spoon and cool.

2. Using a sharp paring knife, peel the fruits. Halve the peaches and remove the pits. Cut each plum into eight wedges and remove the pit.

3. Arrange fruit on a serving platter or on individual dishes. Sprinkle with lime juice and freshly grated nutmeg.

This summer menu is a flamboyant feast for the eyes as well as the palate. The halibut (left) is presented on a plate lined with the outer green leaves of a perfect head of escarole. The inner yellow leaves are used for decoration. After serving the fish, the escarole, tossed with some dressing, becomes a salad. An easy strawberry tart (opposite) makes a colorful finish.

Halibut with Fennel

WE GROW LOTS OF FENNEL— *finocchio*—in the garden. The tops of fennel can be used as an herb for a light anise flavoring, the bulbs for salads, purées, and sauces, and the seeds for Christmas cookies and cakes. The fennel used here is the bulb—julienned very thinly and baked right on top of the halibut steak.

My sister, Laura Herbert, introduced me to green rice. She lived for several years in Tampa, Florida, where lots of rice is consumed by the Cuban population. She tired of white rice and yellow rice and invented green rice. The more herbs you add, the greener the rice. For even more flavor, you can sauté the herbs with onions, shallots, or scallions and add to the cooked rice before serving. You can also add some herbs to the water while the rice is cooking.

The strawberry tart is easy enough to put together, providing you have a tart shell in the freezer. It is that little bit of ahead-of-time planning that makes quick cooking work and appear to be more elaborate than it really is.

❧

MENU
Halibut with Fennel
Green Rice
Tomato, Red Onion, and Fresh Thyme Salad
Strawberry Tart

Halibut with Fennel

SERVES 4

> 3 tablespoons unsalted butter
> 2 shallots, minced (or 2
> tablespoons minced scallions)
> 1 2-pound halibut steak, 1 inch
> thick
> 1 bulb fresh fennel, julienned into
> thin strips
> Juice of 2 lemons
> Salt and freshly ground pepper
> to taste

1. Preheat oven to 375°. Butter a shallow baking dish. Sprinkle shallots over the bottom and put the halibut steak on top. Arrange the fennel strips over the fish, dot with remaining butter, and sprinkle with lemon juice and salt and pepper.

2. Bake for 10 minutes, remove from the oven, and baste fish with cooking juices. Return to the oven and cook for 10 minutes more, or until fish is done (the flesh should be white at the bone). Adjust seasoning and serve.

❧

Green Rice

SERVES 4

> 1 1/2 cups long-grain rice or
> Japanese-style rice
> 6 tablespoons (3/4 stick) unsalted
> butter, melted
> Salt and pepper to taste
> Approximately 1/2 cup each
> finely chopped dill and parsley
> 2 to 3 tablespoons chopped
> scallions or shallots, sautéed in
> butter until soft (optional)

1. Cook rice in a large pot of lightly salted boiling water until tender and fluffy. Taste after 10 minutes and be careful not to overcook.

2. Drain the rice. To serve the rice immediately, put it in a dish and add melted butter. Season lightly with salt and pepper, and toss with herbs and scallions. (If it is to be served later, rinse the rice with cold water, drain well, and set aside. When ready to use, melt the butter in a large skillet, add the rice and scallions, and season with salt and pepper and herbs. Toss well and cook until rice is warm.)

Tomato, Red Onion, and Fresh Thyme Salad

SERVES 4

4 large ripe tomatoes, sliced
1 red onion, thinly sliced
6 sprigs fresh thyme, coarsely
   chopped

VINAIGRETTE (Makes 1/2 cup)

5 tablespoons olive oil
2 tablespoons red wine vinegar
   Salt and pepper to taste

1. Arrange alternating layers of tomato and onion slices on a serving platter. Sprinkle with chopped thyme.

2. Combine ingredients for the vinaigrette and pour dressing over the salad. Serve.

Strawberry Tart

MAKES ONE 7- TO 8-INCH TART

2 pints ripe strawberries
1 cup red currant jelly
2 tablespoons Grand Marnier
   Whipped cream (optional)

SWEET TART CRUST

1 cup flour
1/4 cup sugar
   Pinch of salt
   Rind of 1 orange or lemon,
    grated
4 tablespoons (1/2 stick) unsalted
    butter, cold
1 large egg, slightly beaten

1. To make crust, combine the flour, sugar, salt, and rind in a large mixing bowl. Cut in the butter, 1 tablespoon at a time, using your fingers or an electric mixer, until mixture is crumbly. Add the egg and mix until the dough forms a ball.

2. Roll out the dough into a circle large enough to cover a 7- to 8-inch tart pan. Chill until the shell is stiff, or freeze, well wrapped, for future use.

3. Preheat the oven to 375°. Bake the tart shell until the edges are golden brown, about 20 minutes. Cool on rack.

4. Slice the berries in half lengthwise and arrange on crust as illustrated, in overlapping layers.

5. Melt the currant jelly over low heat and add the Grand Marnier. Cool slightly and brush over the berries, covering the entire surface. Serve plain or with a bowl of whipped cream.

Chicken Salad with Snow Peas and Water Chestnuts

W E ALL LIKE CHICKEN SALAD, and I especially like it made with large pieces of white chicken meat, slightly blanched fresh snow peas, and crispy water chestnuts. You can use leftover roasted chicken for salads, but I prefer freshly poached or baked breasts. Cook whole chicken breasts with skin and bones intact. The result will be juicier and much more flavorful. After removing the meat, use the bones and skin for chicken stock and freeze it in pint and quart amounts for future use.

The dessert, sour cherry clafouti, is a custardlike baked pudding. Almost any summer fruit can be substituted for the sour cherries: dark bing cherries (frozen or canned), sliced peaches, plums, blueberries, or even big plump prunes are delicious. The batter is whipped up in the blender or food processor and the baking takes only 45 minutes. Clafouti should be served warm or at room temperature.

If you have time, bake the orange-raisin muffins. They are wonderful with the chicken salad. I was served these muffins by Gayla Stone, a young teacher of cooking, on a visit to Jackson, Mississippi. They are unusual and the ground raisins and orange peel give them a curiously pleasing texture.

My husband, Andy, is an inveterate collector of bowls. In the background of this picture is a portion of his collection of yellowware. The Oriental-inspired chicken salad is garnished with orange and lime zest and served on an Art Nouveau Limoges platter.

MENU
**Chicken Salad with Snow Peas and Water Chestnuts
Gayla's Orange-Raisin Muffins
Sour Cherry Clafouti**

Chicken Salad with Snow Peas and Water Chestnuts

SERVES 6

2 tablespoons (1/4 stick) unsalted butter
2 whole chicken breasts (from fryer chickens) or 1 breast and 2 thighs *
Salt and pepper to taste
Juice of 1 lemon
1/2 pound snow peas
1 cup sliced canned water chestnuts
Zest of one orange and one lime

DRESSING (Makes 1 cup)

2 tablespoons light soy sauce
1 tablespoon rice vinegar
Zest and juice of 1 lemon
2 tablespoons honey
2 tablespoons chili oil
1/2 cup light vegetable oil
1 tablespoon Szechuan pepper flakes
Salt to taste

1. Preheat oven to 350°. Butter a baking dish.

2. Put the chicken in the baking dish, skin side up. Sprinkle with salt and pepper and lemon juice. Cover tightly with aluminum foil.

3. Bake for 25 to 35 minutes. The meat should be moist.

4. Blanch the snow peas in a large pot of salted boiling water for 30 seconds. Drain and cool them in ice water. Drain again and set aside.

5. Cool the chicken, remove the skin and bones, and shred the meat.

6. Arrange the chicken in a serving bowl with the snow peas and water chestnuts.

7. Combine all ingredients for the dressing and pour it over the salad. Toss well, taste for seasoning, garnish with zest and serve.

* If you have 3 cups of leftover chicken, use this and skip steps 1 through 3.

Gayla's Orange-Raisin Muffins

APPROXIMATELY 30 SMALL OR 16 MEDIUM MUFFINS

1 cup sugar
1/2 cup (1 stick) unsalted butter
2 eggs
1 teaspoon baking soda
1 cup buttermilk
2 cups flour
1/2 teaspoon salt
1 cup raisins
Peel of one orange
Juice of one orange
1/2 cup sugar

1. Preheat oven to 400°. Butter small muffin tins.

2. With an electric mixer, cream the sugar and butter until smooth. Add the eggs and beat until fluffy.

3. Add the baking soda to the buttermilk.

4. Sift the flour and salt together, and add to the sugar-butter-egg mixture alternately with the buttermilk. Stir until mixed.

5. In a food grinder or processor, grind the raisins and orange peel. Add to the batter and combine. Spoon the batter into the prepared muffin tins and bake until golden brown and firm to the touch, about 12 minutes.

6. Remove the tins to a baking rack and set close together. Brush the tops of the muffins with the orange juice and sprinkle with the remaining 1/2 cup sugar while still warm. Cool before serving.

❧

Sour Cherry Clafouti

SERVES 6

> 3 cups pitted fresh sour cherries
>   (canned or frozen may be used)
> 3 tablespoons Cognac
> 1 tablespoon (1/8 stick) unsalted
>   butter
> 1/2 cup sugar
> 3/4 cup milk
> 1/4 cup heavy cream
> 3 eggs
> 1 teaspoon vanilla extract
>   Pinch of salt
> 2/3 cup all-purpose flour

1. Preheat oven to 350°. Combine cherries with Cognac and set aside.

2. Butter a 9-inch glass pie plate or a fluted porcelain tart dish. Dust the bottom with 1 teaspoon sugar.

3. In a blender combine the milk, cream, eggs, remaining sugar, vanilla, salt, and flour. Blend at high speed for 1 minute, scraping the sides of the blender jar once.

4. Pour 1/2 cup batter into the dish. Arrange the cherries over it in an even layer and drizzle with the Cognac. Pour the remaining batter over the cherries.

5. Bake for 45 to 60 minutes, or until the top is puffed and golden brown and the batter is set. Serve hot or warm.

Steamed Shellfish with Herbs

*T*HERE ARE SEVERAL WAYS OF presenting this most unusual and exceedingly simple meal, but each calls for one piece of equipment that is imperative for success in preparation and presentation, namely an Oriental steamer. I prefer bamboo steamers for this meal, primarily because, stacked one atop another, they are more aesthetically pleasing than the metal ones.

My friend Ruth from Los Angeles first introduced me to the following way of serving shellfish. She put one type of fish in each layer and flavored each with a different herb. I take the method one step further and, for the sake of easier serving, put some of each fish in each tray. Almost any fresh herbs will do; I often use fresh basil, chervil, parsley, coriander, and rosemary. Personal preference dictates which fish is flavored with what, but a little experimentation will help you decide.

As the fish steams, carefully move the various layers around so that the fish cooks evenly; as always with fish, it is important not to overcook it. Serve it just cooked, right from the tray, with the various aromas rising in front of each guest. I put each steamer tray directly on a large dinner plate. A bowl for dipping sauce should be served with each tray, and a small waste bowl for shells is a nice touch.

Ruth served tomatoes stuffed with baby string beans—haricots verts—at the same time she showed me the joys of steaming shellfish. She steamed them right in the tomato rings, so that the tomatoes were slightly cooked. I prefer stuffing the rings with the blanched beans and serving the "salad" with a rich vinaigrette.

For dessert, present your family and guests with raspberry-stuffed figs served with raspberry sauce and a dollop of crème fraîche.

*In one layer of an Oriental steamer (**opposite**), fresh thyme mingles with scallops, sprigs of oregano with unshelled shrimp, variegated sage with little-neck clams, and fresh dill with scrubbed mussels. **Above:** an unusual salad presentation of baby string beans stuffed into fresh tomato rings and dressed with a rich, mustardy vinaigrette.*

MENU
Steamed Shellfish with Herbs
Ginger-Soy Sauce
Tomatoes Stuffed with Baby String Beans
Figs Stuffed with Raspberries

Steamed Shellfish with Herbs

TWO DOZEN SHELLFISH PER PERSON

GINGER-SOY SAUCE (Makes 1/2 cup)

1/2 cup light soy sauce
1 tablespoon Japanese rice vinegar
1/2 teaspoon hot sesame oil
1 teaspoon chives or scallions, minced
1/2 teaspoon grated fresh ginger

6 cherrystone clams, washed
6 mussels, scrubbed
4 to 6 large shrimp in shells
4 to 6 large sea scallops
Small bunches of fresh herbs such as dill, oregano, thyme, basil, sage, chervil, parsley

1. In a small serving bowl combine all the ingredients for the ginger-soy sauce. Set aside.

2. For each serving, in one tier of a multilayered steamer arrange an assortment of shellfish as pictured. Season each type of shellfish with a different herb according to your preference.

3. Place the steamer in a large skillet filled with boiling water that reaches halfway up the lowest level of the steamer. Steam over high heat for 3 minutes.

4. Switch steamer baskets, putting the lowest layer on top. Cook 3 minutes and switch again. Remove the layers as the shellfish are cooked. (Clams and mussels will open and shrimp will turn pink.) Be careful not to overcook.

5. Serve each person one tray of the steamer on a large dinner plate, along with a bowl of dipping sauce.

Note: I find that four layers stacked on top of each other is maximum for easy handling and satisfactory results. If you plan on serving more guests, use another steamer set over another pan of boiling water.

Tomatoes Stuffed with Baby String Beans

1 TOMATO PER PERSON

1 tomato
12 to 14 haricots verts (very thin
    string beans)

RICH VINAIGRETTE
(Makes 1 1/2 cups)

3/4 cup light olive oil
1/3 cup red wine vinegar
1 tablespoon Dijon mustard
Salt and pepper to taste

1. Combine all the vinaigrette ingredients in a bowl. Stir well and set aside.

2. Slice off the top and bottom of the tomato. With a small spoon remove the seeds and the inside pulp so you are left with a ring of flesh and skin, as shown. Set aside.

3. Cut off stem end of the haricots verts and wash them. Put the beans in a steamer and cook for 3 to 5 minutes. Do not overcook.

4. Put the warm haricots verts in the tomato ring. Serve hot or warm with the rich vinaigrette.

Figs Stuffed with Raspberries

1 FIG PER PERSON

1 to 2 large fresh figs
1/2 pint ripe raspberries

RASPBERRY SAUCE
(Makes 2 cups)

1 quart fresh raspberries or two
    12-ounce packages frozen
    raspberries
3/4 cup sugar
3 tablespoons Grand Marnier
    Crème fraîche (optional)

1. Slice the figs into sixths, cutting from the top to within 1 inch of the bottom. Spread the segments open like a flower, making sure not to break them. Fill the center of each with raspberries.

2. To make the sauce, press the 1 quart berries through a fine sieve. Mix the purée with the sugar and Grand Marnier until the sugar is all dissolved. Chill until ready to use.

3. To serve, spoon raspberry sauce over the figs and garnish with crème fraîche if desired.

Grilled Red Snapper with Tarragon Butter

*T*HIS MENU WILL DELIGHT ANY-
one who is fond of fish. I grill red snapper over hickory or mesquite, and
the result is extraordinary. The slight smokiness of the fire flavors the delicate fish, and the herbs—dill and tarragon—add a special fragrance. This is
certainly an easy way to cook snapper, and also whole bluefish, salmon, or
bass. Tie the fish closed with twine made of natural fibers, and turn very
carefully with large spatulas so that the skin does not break too much while
grilling. If you own a fish grill—one that encloses the fish—use it, for it
makes turning the fish simple. It is important to use a grill that is quite fine;
wide spaces will cause the fish to break when turned.

Yellow squash, one of those abundant summer vegetables that can
taste bland, is very delicious here sautéed in oil and served with fresh rosemary and *pumate,* sun-dried tomatoes in olive oil imported from Italy.

The salad of fresh spinach leaves and ruby red grapefruit sections
served with a sweet vinegar–poppy seed dressing is refreshing and unusual.
When buying fresh spinach, select young leaves that have not been crushed
or bruised. The prewashed, packaged spinach is perfectly satisfactory for
cooked dishes but not very good for a raw salad such as this. In general, I
find that Oriental vegetable markets treat fresh spinach with greater respect
than American markets; they always seem to have whole, tender leaves
nicely tied into bunches.

*Whole fish, simply grilled
with fresh herbs and
served with an herb-
flavored butter, is for me
one of the real delights of
summer cooking. Yellow
summer squash and a
salad with an unusual
poppyseed dressing are
served from New England
salt-glaze pie plates.*

❧

MENU
Grilled Red Snapper with Tarragon Butter
Summer Squash with Sun-Dried Tomatoes
Spinach and Ruby Red Grapefruit Salad
Iced Bing Cherries and Cookies

Grilled Red Snapper with Tarragon Butter

SERVES 4

TARRAGON BUTTER (Makes 1/2 cup)

2 tablespoons champagne or white
   wine vinegar
4 tablespoons white wine
8 tablespoons (1 stick) cold
   unsalted butter
   Salt to taste
8 to 10 leaves fresh tarragon,
   chopped

2 red snappers (1 3/4 to 2 pounds
   each)
2 medium-size bunches dill
   Sprigs of fresh tarragon, to taste
4 tablespoons vegetable oil
   Salt and pepper to taste

1. To make tarragon butter, in a saucepan combine vinegar and white wine. Bring to a boil and reduce to a third of the volume. Remove from heat and whisk in butter, 1 tablespoon at a time, until all is incorporated. Add salt and tarragon leaves.

2. Stuff the red snappers with dill and tarragon. Tie the fish shut with twine.

3. Brush fish with oil and grill over hot coals, or under a hot broiler, for 10 to 12 minutes, turning once or twice. Do not overcook. Serve immediately with tarragon butter and salt and pepper.

Summer Squash with Sun-Dried Tomatoes

SERVES 4

3 to 4 yellow squashes
4 sun-dried tomatoes (pumate)
2 tablespoons oil from the
   tomatoes
4 sprigs fresh rosemary
   Salt and pepper to taste

1. Slice squash into round or diagonal pieces about 1/4 inch thick.

2. Slice tomatoes into thin strips.

3. In a skillet heat oil over high heat and sauté squash slices on both sides until light brown. Add tomato strips, rosemary, and salt and pepper. Toss well. Serve immediately.

Spinach and Ruby Red Grapefruit Salad

SERVES 4

POPPY SEED DRESSING*
(Makes 1 1/2 cups)

3 tablespoons champagne or white
  wine vinegar
3 tablespoons honey
  Juice of 1 lemon
1/4 cup olive oil
1/2 cup vegetable oil
1/4 cup poppy seeds
1 teaspoon pepper
  Salt to taste

2 pounds fresh spinach
1 ruby red grapefruit

1. Combine all the dressing ingredients. Mix thoroughly and refrigerate until ready to use.

2. Wash, stem, and dry the spinach. Put in a large salad bowl.

3. Peel and section the grapefruit and combine with the spinach in a bowl. Pour the dressing over the salad and toss gently.

  * This makes more than enough for the salad. Whatever is left over can be stored, refrigerated, for up to a week.

Iced Bing Cherries and Cookies

Fill a large bowl with ice cubes and add 1 to 2 pounds dark, firm Bing cherries. Served this way, the cherries will stay deliciously cold and are fun to eat.
  Serve with large sugared sables or butter cookies.

This menu is one I cook over and over again when soft-shell crabs are in season. Here, the crabs are nestled with sautéed julienned Japanese eggplant and angle-cut scallions on a nineteenth-century hand-painted Limoges platter. Cold spicy sesame noodles (above) are the perfect accompaniment. I like to use a curly pasta called fusilli, but buckwheat noodles, vermicelli, or other egg pastas work equally well. The sesame seeds for this dish may be ground with a mortar and pestle for a finer texture after they are toasted.

✿

MENU
Soft-Shell Crabs
Spicy Sesame Noodles
Eggplant with Scallions
Honeydew Melon

$\int$ *O F T - S H E L L   C R A B S   A R E*
actually blue crabs that have molted and are growing new shells, which for a very short time each spring and summer are soft enough to be eaten completely with the crab meat when properly cooked.

Soft-shell crabs, which are shipped live, packed in seaweed, from the Chesapeake or the Gulf, must be cleaned before cooking. Get instructions from your fishmonger on how to remove the eyes and gills from under the shell, or ask him to do it for you. This should be done not longer than three to four hours before using the crabs.

I also have successfully frozen soft-shell crabs. They must be cleaned and frozen in one layer in sheets of ice. Simply arrange the crabs in a shallow dish, cover with water, and freeze. When hard, remove from dish and wrap very well. Thaw in the refrigerator overnight and use as you would fresh crabs.

✿

Spicy Sesame Noodles
SERVES 4

3 *to 4 scallions*
8 *ounces egg or buckwheat pasta*
2 *tablespoons toasted sesame seeds (see page 108)*

DRESSING

3 *tablespoons rice vinegar*
1 *tablespoon sesame paste*
2 *tablespoons peanut butter*
1 *tablespoon honey mustard (or 2 teaspoons each honey and Dijon mustard)*
2 *tablespoons soy sauce*
1 *tablespoon chili oil*
1/3 *cup sesame oil*
1/4 *cup vegetable oil*
Juice of 1/2 orange or tangerine
Salt and pepper to taste

1. Cut the scallions into 2 1/2-inch pieces. Sliver as pictured to make "brushes." Place in ice water and set aside.

2. In a mixing bowl combine vinegar, sesame paste, peanut butter, honey mustard, and soy sauce. Combine the oils and add to mixing bowl slowly, whisking as you would to make mayonnaise. Add orange juice and salt and pepper. For a spicier dressing add a few more drops of the hot oil. Set aside.

3. Cook pasta in a large kettle of boiling water according to directions on the package, or to taste. Drain pasta in a colander and run cold water over it. Drain well.

4. In a large bowl toss noodles with the dressing, drained scallions, and sesame seeds. Chill for at least 30 minutes before serving.

✻

Soft-Shell Crabs

SERVES 4

8 to 12 soft-shell crabs
1 cup flour
Salt and freshly ground pepper
    to taste
Large pinch of cayenne pepper
4 to 6 sprigs fresh thyme
Light oil for sautéing (olive oil or
    blended oil)
1 tablespoon chopped parsley
Lemon wedges

1. Clean and rinse the crabs. Drain. Dredge the crabs lightly in flour and shake off the excess. Sprinkle with salt and pepper and cayenne pepper and insert a small piece of thyme under the shell of each crab.

2. In a large skillet heat 1/3 inch oil until it is very hot but not smoking. Put the crabs in the hot oil, belly down. Sauté for 3 minutes. Turn the crabs and cook for about 4 minutes more.

3. Remove crabs from the pan, drain on paper towels, sprinkle with parsley, and serve hot with lemon wedges.

✻

Eggplant with Scallions

SERVES 4

5 Japanese eggplants (the long,
    light purple variety, if possible)
    or 8 small dark purple Italian
    eggplants
1 tablespoon salt
4 tablespoons vegetable oil or
    peanut oil
4 scallions, cut into 3/4-inch pieces
    on the diagonal
Black pepper to taste

1. Slice eggplants lengthwise into 1/2-inch by 2 1/2-inch pieces, put in a colander, and sprinkle with salt. Let stand for 15 to 20 minutes. Rinse and pat dry.

2. In a large skillet heat oil and sauté the eggplant 3 to 5 minutes, or until tender and golden brown. Just before removing eggplant from the heat, add the scallions and toss lightly. Season with pepper. Serve immediately.

A summertime version of borscht (opposite), garnished with a sprig of dill, looks wonderfully refreshing in opalescent Fire King Depression-era bowls. **Left:** one of Andy's favorite Quick Cook meals, herb-sautéed pork chops with Granny Smith apples.

Thyme-Sautéed Pork Chops with Apple Slices

I MAKE THIS MENU JUST AS the first beets and zucchini are being picked from the garden. The soup is a hearty borscht in which all of the vegetables are cooked just until tender.

The pork chops should be cut extra-thin (1/2 inch) so that they can cook very fast. Fresh thyme is put right under the chop, where it sticks while cooking. Herbs sautéed in this way are delicious. Apple slices are sautéed in the same pan after the chops are done.

I like to grow a great variety of salad greens in the greenhouse in winter and in the garden during the summer and pick it while it is still very young and tender. I often let butter lettuce get just large enough so that one head is a salad for each person. Whole, small lettuces are also nice "bowls" for summer salads made of sweet corn, seafood or chicken.

Another thing I grow lots of are raspberries. There are five long rows in the garden—about five varieties—and I harvest glorious berries all summer and fall. Fresh raspberries, served with dollops of raspberry cream, make a luscious ending to this meal.

❦

MENU
Beet-Zucchini Soup
Thyme-Sautéed Pork Chops with Apple Slices
Salad of Young Lettuces
Raspberries and Cream

Beet-Zucchini Soup

1 pound beets, peeled and grated
1/4 cup red wine vinegar
　Pinch of sugar
4 tablespoons (1/2 stick) unsalted
　butter
1 tablespoon vegetable oil
1 large onion, sliced
2 scallions, chopped
2 carrots, peeled and thinly sliced
1 apple, peeled and thinly sliced
1 pound green cabbage, thinly
　sliced
2 small zucchini, sliced
4 cups homemade beef, veal, or
　chicken stock
　Salt and pepper to taste
　Sour cream or crème fraîche
　(optional)
　Sprig of fresh dill (optional)

1. Soak a third of the grated beets in vinegar and sugar. Set aside.

2. Heat the butter and oil in a large soup kettle. Sauté the onion and scallions over medium heat until soft, about 5 minutes. Add the remaining beets, carrots, and apple and cook until tender, 15 to 20 minutes.

3. Add the cabbage and zucchini to the pot and cook for 3 minutes.

4. In a separate pot, bring the stock to a boil. Pour it over the vegetables and cook over medium heat for 5 to 10 minutes. The cabbage and zucchini should be cooked but still firm.

5. Add the beets and vinegar. Season with salt and pepper. This soup can be served hot, warm, or cold, with a dollop of sour cream or crème fraîche if desired, and garnished with a sprig of fresh dill.

❧

Salad of Young Lettuces

SERVES 4 TO 6

Allow a handful of young lettuces, such as Bibb, Boston, salad bowl, or ruby, per person

LIGHT VINAIGRETTE
(Makes 3/4 cup)

3 tablespoons Japanese rice
　vinegar
1/2 cup safflower oil
　Salt and pepper to taste
1 tablespoon finely chopped
　parsley

1. Arrange the lettuces in a large salad bowl.

2. In a small mixing bowl combine all ingredients for the vinaigrette. Stir well and pour over the lettuce. Toss and serve.

❦

Thyme-Sautéed Pork Chops with Apple Slices

SERVES 4 TO 6

> 1/2 **cup flour**
> **Salt and pepper to taste**
> 8 **extra-thin (1/2-inch thick) loin**
> **pork chops**
> 4 **tablespoons (1/2 stick) unsalted**
> **butter**
> 4 **tablespoons olive oil**
> 16 **sprigs fresh thyme, or 2**
> **tablespoons dried thyme**
> 2 **Granny Smith or McIntosh**
> **apples, unpeeled, cut in**
> **1/4-inch slices**

1. Combine the flour with salt and pepper. Lightly dredge the pork chops in the flour.

2. Heat half the butter and oil in a large skillet. Sauté half the chops for 5 minutes on each side. While the chops are cooking, put some of the thyme under each chop so the herb will stick to the meat. Remove the chops and keep warm.

3. Add the remaining oil and butter to the skillet and cook the rest of the chops the same way. Remove them and keep warm.

4. Using the same skillet, sauté the apples for 2 to 4 minutes, or until soft but not mushy. Arrange the chops and apples on a serving dish.

❦

Raspberries and Cream

SERVES 4 TO 6

> 1 **cup heavy cream**
> 1/4 **teaspoon vanilla extract**
> 1 **tablespoon sugar**
> 2 **pints fresh raspberries**

1. Whip the cream, vanilla, and sugar until it forms soft peaks. With a spoon, stir in a quarter of the raspberries, crushing them. (The cream will become pink.)

2. Arrange the remaining berries in 4 small serving bowls and top with the raspberry cream.

Shrimp Chinoise

SARA FOSTER, MY CATERING
chef and a very talented, inventive young woman, created shrimp Chinoise, which has become one of our most popular summer salads. Sara always uses very large shrimp in this salad. She cooks the shrimp unpeeled, cools them, then peels off the shell very carefully so that the tail is left intact. Each vegetable is prepared and kept separate until the salad is tossed with the unusual sesame dressing. Along with the salad I suggest serving Japanese-inspired cold buckwheat noodles.

Begin the meal with a frozen pineapple daiquiri. If you prefer, you can omit the rum. The drink is quite thick, so I like to serve it in a stemmed goblet with a small silver teaspoon.

For dessert, serve iced watermelon in thick slices or wedges. When choosing watermelon, look for half of a melon that has a rich, sweet fragrance and bright red color.

Note: This menu calls for a number of ingredients—sesame oil, hot chili oil, black soy sauce, buckwheat noodles—which are not generally found in ordinary supermarkets. It is wise, therefore, to have a supply of these unusual items in the pantry. Buy small jars, bottles, and cans, and more than one of each so that they will have less chance of going stale if you use them infrequently. I keep a list of such ingredients and whenever I am in Chinatown, or in an Oriental market, I purchase what I need.

This Chinese-inspired summer salad, with snow peas, carrots, cauliflower, broccoli, Shitake mushrooms, bok choy cabbage, red peppers, and shrimp sprinkled with toasted sesame seeds, looks best in an etched, cut-glass bowl.

MENU
Frozen Pineapple Daiquiri
Shrimp Chinoise
Cold Buckwheat Noodles
Iced Watermelon

Frozen Pineapple Daiquiri

1/2 cup unsweetened pineapple juice
1 ounce light rum
Juice of 1/2 lime
1 tablespoon coconut cream
6 ice cubes
Small piece of fresh pineapple

1. Put all the ingredients in a blender. Blend until the ice is finely crushed.

2. Serve in an iced goblet.

Shrimp Chinoise

SERVES 6 TO 8

2 pounds jumbo shrimps, unpeeled
1/2 pound snow peas, strings removed
1/2 pound carrots, peeled and cut diagonally into 2-inch pieces
1/2 head cauliflower, cut into flowerets
1/2 head broccoli, cut into flowerets
1/4 pound shitake mushrooms, cleaned and sliced
1 cup bok choy cabbage, cut into 1 1/2-inch pieces
3 red peppers, seeded and cut into thin strips

DRESSING

2 tablespoons Japanese rice vinegar
1 tablespoon cider vinegar
1 tablespoon chili oil
2 tablespoons soy sauce
1/2 cup sesame oil
1 cup vegetable oil
2 cloves garlic, finely minced
Juice of 1 lemon or orange
1 teaspoon Dijon mustard
1 tablespoon honey
1/4 cup toasted sesame seeds *

1. Drop shrimp in a large kettle of rapidly boiling salted water and cook for 3 to 4 minutes, or until the shrimp turn pink. Drain and run them under cold water to cool. Peel the shrimp, leaving the tail attached if possible. Refrigerate.

2. In separate pots of boiling water blanch the snow peas for 30 seconds, the carrots 3 minutes, the cauliflower 4 minutes, and the broccoli 4 minutes. Remove vegetables with a slotted spoon or Chinese strainer and put them in ice water to stop cooking. Drain and set aside. The vegetables should still be crunchy.

3. Combine all the ingredients for the dressing in a small mixing bowl.

4. In a large bowl combine the shrimps, cooked vegetables, mushrooms, cabbage, and red peppers. Pour on dressing, toss well, and refrigerate for at least 1 hour. Serve cold.

* To toast sesame seeds, place seeds in a hot fry pan and toss gently over high heat until they are lightly toasted.

Cold Buckwheat Noodles

SERVES 6

1 pound buckwheat noodles
2 tablespoons sesame oil
3 tablespoons thinly sliced
  scallions
2 tablespoons peanut oil
1 tablespoon hot chili oil
3 1/2 tablespoons black soy sauce
1 1/2 tablespoons Chinese black
  vinegar or balsamic vinegar
1 tablespoon sugar
Salt to taste

1. Cook the noodles in a large pot of boiling lightly salted water until tender, about 10 minutes. Drain and rinse under cold running water. Drain well and toss with the sesame oil. Set aside.

2. In a mixing bowl combine the scallions, peanut oil, chili oil, soy sauce, vinegar, and sugar. Pour over the noodles and toss well. Taste for seasoning. Let stand for 1 hour before serving to allow flavors to blend.

Iced Watermelon

SERVES 6

1/2 large, ripe watermelon
Coarse salt
2 limes, cut into wedges

1. Keep the watermelon well refrigerated or on ice until serving time.

2. Cut the watermelon into slices or wedges with a sharp knife. I like to serve it on dessert plates with small forks and fruit knives, accompanied by coarse salt and wedges of lime.

Red Snapper Baked in Parchment

I WAS FIRST SERVED SNAPPER baked in parchment in a charming restaurant called La Tulipe in New York City. The presentation was so lovely—a large puffy package of parchment paper enclosing a perfectly cooked fillet of red snapper and a mélange of baby vegetables lightly seasoned with thyme and dill and butter. It is quite spectacular and very easy to re-create at home. Parchment is available by the roll or sheet in gourmet cooking shops or bakery supply houses.

Sorrel is a little-known green but one that has many uses. It is easily grown—one variety is a common American weed—and produces sour, tart leaves almost all year long. It is the last plant to die in the fall and the very first to produce leaves in the spring. I use sorrel not only for soups but also as a flavoring for sauces for fish, as a chiffonade atop fish, and as an addition to some vegetable purées. In Europe almost every country has its version of sour-grass soup. My version is basically a French soup to which egg yolks and cream are added at the last moment. Sorrel soup is excellent served hot, but equally interesting served cold with an enrichment of crème fraîche.

The dessert is a rich chocolate mousse with a fresh mint taste invented by my pastry chef, Jane Stacey. Serve it in glass goblets or on clear glass dessert plates with generous helpings of freshly whipped cream. Decorate the mousse with fresh mint leaves if you have some available.

The red snapper, in its puff of parchment, is surrounded by baby carrots, potatoes, turnips, cucumber, and fresh dill and served on individual red-ware plates. I frequently like to use large linen dishtowels as placemats for a summer table; they are colorful and easy to care for.

❦

MENU
Cold Sorrel Soup
Red Snapper Baked in Parchment
Cucumber Salad
Minted Chocolate Mousse

Cold Sorrel Soup

SERVES 4

4 cups packed sorrel leaves
(choose the small, tender leaves)
4 cups boiling chicken stock
2 tablespoons (1/4 stick) unsalted
butter
1/2 cup minced scallions
2 tablespoons all-purpose flour
2 egg yolks
1/2 to 3/4 cup light cream (to taste)
Salt to taste
Crème fraîche to taste (see page
17)
Chopped chervil or summer
savory to taste

1. Cut the sorrel leaves into fine, long strips (chiffonade). Set aside.

2. In a large pot melt the butter and sauté the scallions over medium heat until soft but not browned, about 5 minutes.

3. Add the sorrel and cook until wilted. Stir in the flour and cook for 3 minutes.

4. Stir in the boiling stock, reduce heat, and simmer for 5 minutes. Remove from heat.

5. In a mixing bowl combine the egg yolks and cream. Whisking constantly, add 1 cup of the hot soup, a drop at a time (to keep the eggs from curdling). Pour this mixture back into the soup, stir well, and season.

6. Let soup cool to room temperature, then chill. Serve the soup with a dollop of crème fraîche and a sprinkling of fresh herb.

Red Snapper Baked in Parchment

SERVES 4

Parchment paper
4 tablespoons (1/2 stick) unsalted
butter
4 red snapper fillets
2 small potatoes, each peeled and
cut into eighths
8 baby turnips, trimmed and
sliced
8 baby carrots, peeled and cut in
half lengthwise
4 sprigs thyme
4 sprigs dill
Salt and pepper to taste

1. Preheat oven to 350°. Cut four circles of parchment paper 14 to 16 inches in diameter. Butter one side of each circle.

2. Put each fish fillet on one half of the buttered side of the parchment circles. Distribute the vegetables and herbs over the fish. Sprinkle with salt and pepper. Dot fish with remaining butter. Fold over the parchment and crimp the edges to seal.

3. Bake until the parchment has puffed, about 12 minutes. The fish should be done and the vegetables should be crisp. Serve immediately, and let your guests break open the parchment.

❧

Cucumber Salad

SERVES 4

Score 2 unpeeled seedless cucumbers by running a fork along them length-wise. Slice them, crosswise, very thinly. In a bowl combine 4 tablespoons Japanese rice vinegar, 1 teaspoon sugar, 6 tablespoons crème fraîche (see page 17), and 1 tablespoon chopped fresh dill. Add the cucumbers, toss, and chill until ready to serve.

❧

Minted Chocolate Mousse

SERVES 4 TO 6

> 6 ounces semisweet chocolate
> 3 eggs, separated
> 1 to 2 tablespoons sugar, to taste
> 3/4 cup heavy cream
> 1/2 teaspoon mint extract (or 1
>   tablespoon crème de menthe or
>   2 tablespoons chopped fresh
>   mint leaves)
> Whipped cream (optional)

1. Melt the chocolate in a double boiler over simmering water. Remove from the heat and pour into a mixing bowl.

2. Lightly beat the egg yolks and blend them into the chocolate.

3. In a separate bowl beat the egg whites to a soft peak. Add sugar and beat again to form stiff peaks.

4. Mix a third of the whites into the chocolate mixture and then fold the chocolate into the remaining beaten whites, a little at a time.

5. Whip the heavy cream with the mint extract until stiff and fold into the chocolate mixture. Chill thoroughly. Top with whipped cream, if desired.

This kind of salade composée can be made at any time during the summer when there is an abundance and variety of garden-fresh vegetables. Here, cherry tomatoes, green beans, yellow wax beans, new potatoes, and scallions are arranged with chunks of flavorful Italian tuna, quartered hard-boiled eggs, anchovies, capers, and olives on a Shaker-style cherrywood tray. The vinaigrette dressing is served on the side from a small yellowware bowl.

MENU

Salade Niçoise à la Middlefield
Crispy French Bread
Fresh Fruit Salad

*S*EVENTEEN YEARS AGO ANDY and I bought our first house in the Berkshire mountains in Middlefield, Massachusetts. It was a 150-year-old schoolhouse on a deserted dirt road in the middle of nowhere, but we had a four-acre field of rich bottomland, a virgin hemlock forest, two mountain streams with good clear water, and innumerable swimming holes. Here, Andy learned carpentry, plumbing, ditch digging, and gardening; I became an excellent house painter, landscape architect, iron-stove chef, and basic jack-of-all trades. We plowed a great big garden in Middlefield and planted an orchard. Everything grew fantastically—the combination of naturally rich loam, plenty of water, and warm days and cool nights created an ideal environment. Every Sunday evening we lugged back bushels of fresh produce for ourselves and our friends in New York.

The following menu is typical of what we ate every weekend of the summer: a salad composed of vegetables and herbs from the garden, eggs from the six hens we kept each summer, and a few exotic things we imported from New York. Middlefield had only one general store, which sold more farming equipment and Wonder Bread than anything else, but we could buy fine fresh blueberries and peaches, which were the basis for the fruit salads we loved to eat for dessert.

Salade Niçoise à la Middlefield
SERVES 4 TO 6

VINAIGRETTE (Makes 1 cup)

2/3 cup olive oil
1 tablespoon lemon juice
3 tablespoons wine vinegar
2 tablespoons Dijon mustard
1 clove garlic, minced
1 tablespoon chopped fresh basil
1 tablespoon chopped fresh parsley (and/or dill)
Salt and pepper to taste

8 new potatoes
1 tablespoon minced scallions
3 tablespoons dry vermouth
Salt and pepper to taste
1/2 pound green beans
2 large heads Boston or Bibb lettuce, washed, with leaves left whole
4 ripe tomatoes, quartered (or 12 cherry tomatoes, halved)
2 7-ounce tins Italian tuna, drained
3 tablespoons tiny capers
1/2 cup Niçoise olives (available in specialty stores)
1 2-ounce tin rolled anchovies
3 hard-boiled eggs, peeled and halved

1. Combine vinaigrette ingredients in a small mixing bowl. Set aside until ready to use.

2. Steam the potatoes until tender, about 15 to 20 minutes. Peel and slice them. Toss slices with scallions, vermouth, and salt and pepper. Set aside.

3. Blanch green beans in 3 quarts salted boiling water for 3 to 5 minutes. Drain and chill them in ice water. Drain again and dry well.

4. Toss the lettuce with 2 tablespoons of the vinaigrette. Arrange the leaves at the bottom of a deep, round platter.

5. Put the potato slices in a ring on top of the lettuce and arrange the beans and tomatoes in a decorative pattern.

6. Flake the tuna into a mound in the center of the dish. Sprinkle capers and olives over it.

7. Put the anchovies on top of the halved eggs and arrange them around the tuna. Spoon the dressing over the salad and serve at once.

Fresh Fruit Salad

SERVES 4 TO 6

> 2 *pints blueberries*
> 1/2 *pound large Bing cherries,*
>   *halved and pitted*
> 4 *large peaches, sliced*
> 1/4 *cup Grand Marnier*
> 1/4 *cup sugar*
> 1 *pint fresh raspberries*
>   *Vanilla yogurt (optional)*

1. Toss the blueberries, cherries, and peaches with Grand Marnier and sugar.

2. Put the fruit in a clear glass bowl and sprinkle raspberries over everything. Serve plain or with chilled vanilla yogurt.

Fall

Frittata

*Y*EARS AGO, WHEN ANDY AND I visited Spain and the Balearic Islands, we discovered in Ibiza what the natives called frittatas—huge thick omelettes baked in the oven and filled with potatoes, onions, sometimes chorizo, peppers, and olives. Because we were on an extremely tight travel budget, a great chunk of frittata accompanied by oil-soaked peasant bread frequently comprised our lunches on that lovely isle.

Since we raise our own hens and have numerous eggs, frittatas remain one of our staple foods. I often serve a frittata for a lunch or supper, using as filling whatever vegetables and meats I have on hand—zucchini, eggplants, tomatoes, potatoes, onions, or peppers, as well as grated cheeses, olives, artichoke hearts, asparagus spears, or sausage of some type. I bake the frittata in a very hot oven so that the bottom and sides cook quickly and brown and the top becomes puffy. I use either an ovenproof frying pan (cast iron is good) or a large tin-lined copper pan that holds a 12-egg filling.

For dessert, baked apricots, cooked while the omelette is puffing, are quick and good. Fresh, unpeeled freestone peaches could be used instead of apricots.

As I feed the chickens in the background, one of my helpers, Celia, is breaking the eggs for a fluffy 12-egg frittata.

MENU
Littleneck Clams on the Half Shell
Frittata
Hot Crispy Breads
Salad of Arugula and Cherry Tomatoes
Baked Apricots

Littleneck Clams on the Half Shell

Allowing at least 6 clams per person, top each with a bit of spicy Chinese chili paste and finely chopped scallions and serve with lemon wedges.

❧

Frittata

SERVES 6

2 small-size eggplants, thinly sliced
1/2 teaspoon salt
1/2 cup olive oil
2 baking potatoes, peeled and thinly sliced
1 large onion, peeled and thinly sliced
2 small zucchini, thinly sliced
2 red peppers, minced
12 eggs
Salt and pepper to taste
Sprigs of fresh thyme to taste

1. Preheat the oven to 450°. Sprinkle the eggplants with salt, put in a colander, and let stand for 10 minutes. Rinse with cold water and pat dry.

2. Pour the olive oil into a 12-inch baking dish. Heat the oil in the oven for 5 minutes and remove.

3. Arrange the potato and onion slices in the baking dish and bake for 20 minutes, or until the potatoes are slightly tender.

4. Arrange the zucchini and eggplant slices on top of the potatoes and bake for 5 minutes.

5. Sprinkle the red peppers over the other vegetables. Beat the eggs and season with salt and pepper. Pour the eggs over the vegetables and arrange the thyme on top. Bake until the eggs are set and the sides have puffed, about 20 minutes. (Reduce oven temperature if eggs cook too fast.) The top will become golden brown and a knife inserted in the middle should come out clean. Do not overcook. The frittata should be firm but not dry. Serve hot or at room temperature.

Salad of Arugula and Cherry Tomatoes

SERVES 6

**Allow a small handful of
arugula and 4 to 6 cherry
tomatoes per person**

**CREAMY GORGONZOLA VINAIGRETTE
(Makes 1¹/₃ cups)**

2 tablespoons Dijon mustard
1/3 cup tarragon vinegar
2/3 cup olive oil
1/3 cup crumbled Gorgonzola cheese
1 tablespoon lemon juice
Freshly ground black pepper

1. Wash arugula carefully and dry well. Cut tomatoes in half.

2. Put the arugula and the cherry tomatoes in a large salad bowl.

3. Combine all the ingredients for the vinaigrette. Pour over the salad, toss well, and serve immediately.

Baked Apricots

SERVES 6

12 fresh apricots, halved and pitted
1/4 cup water
1/4 cup vanilla-flavored sugar*
Plain yogurt or heavy cream

1. Preheat the oven to 375°. Put the apricot halves in a baking dish, cut side down, and add the water. Sprinkle the apricots with sugar.

2. Bake for 30 to 40 minutes, or until the apricots are soft but not mushy. Serve with yogurt or cream.

  * To make vanilla-flavored sugar, store a few vanilla beans in a jar of sugar for several weeks. Add more sugar to the jar as you need it. Vanilla-flavored sugar will keep indefinitely in the refrigerator and can be used for many desserts.

An old English bread-board is used to serve a different, very easy apple pie (opposite). A circle of pastry dough several inches larger than the pie plate is filled with apples and spices, and then the edges are simply folded up and over the fruit and baked. A small yellowware bowl holds freshly whipped cream. Left: the colorful main course is served from a pottery plate made by my daughter Alexis.

Sesame Chicken in Acorn Squash

❧

MENU
Bibb Lettuce Salad
with Grilled Brie on French Bread
Sesame Chicken in Acorn Squash
Old-fashioned Bottom-Crust Apple Pie

acorn squash is the colorful, very autumnal basis for this menu. We are accustomed to baked acorn squash with brown sugar, butter, and bacon, or steamed squash with nothing but salt and pepper and butter. In this recipe the squash halves are filled with crunchy sesame chicken strips and Chinese vegetables prepared while the squash bakes. Grilled Brie cheese on thin slices of French bread is delicious served as an hors d'oeuvre with cocktails before dinner, or as a first course, with soft Bibb lettuce salad.

To make the old-fashioned bottom-crust apple pie, you need to have a circle of pie crust in your freezer and some good tart apples in the pantry. I make pie pastry every so often and roll out 12-inch circles, then freeze these circles between pieces of plastic wrap, to use as needed.

Bibb Lettuce Salad with Grilled Brie on French Bread

SERVES 4

Arrange 4 small whole heads of Bibb lettuce on individual serving plates that you have rubbed with a split garlic clove. Sprinkle each to taste with a bit of olive oil, lemon juice, and freshly ground black pepper.

To make the grilled Brie, slice one small loaf of French bread diagonally into 3/4-inch pieces. (You should allow 3 to 4 pieces per person.) Spread each slice of bread with softened unsalted butter and Dijon mustard, and cover with thin slices of Brie cheese. Put under a preheated broiler for 2 minutes, until the cheese is hot and bubbly. Serve immediately alongside the salad with a sprinkling of finely chopped chervil or parsley.

Sesame Chicken in Acorn Squash

SERVES 4

MARINADE

1 1-inch piece fresh ginger, peeled and thinly sliced
2 tablespoons sesame oil
3 cloves garlic, peeled and split
Pinch of dried chili pepper or 1 fresh chili, minced
1 teaspoon chili powder
1/2 cup white wine
1/4 cup soy sauce

2 whole chicken breasts, boned, skinned, and cut into 3/4-inch strips
2 acorn squash, halved lengthwise
1/2 cup flour
2 tablespoons black sesame seeds
2 tablespoons white sesame seeds
3 tablespoons unsalted butter
3 carrots, peeled, sliced, and blanched
20 snow peas, blanched
1 small head broccoli, cut into small flowerets, blanched

1. Mix all marinade ingredients in a bowl. Put the chicken in the marinade and let it sit overnight, preferably, or at least 30 minutes.

2. Preheat oven to 350°. Put squash halves, cut side down, in a baking pan. Add 1/2 inch water and bake until squash are tender, 30 to 40 minutes.

3. About 15 minutes before the squash is done, combine flour and sesame seeds. Roll chicken strips in the mixture.

4. Melt butter in a skillet and sauté chicken for 4 to 5 minutes, until golden. Remove chicken and set aside. Pour off excess butter and crumbs.

5. Deglaze the skillet with 1/4 cup of the strained marinade. Add carrots, snow peas, and broccoli and cook just enough to heat the vegetables.

6. Add the chicken strips and toss well. Serve the chicken and vegetables spilling over the squash halves.

Old-fashioned Bottom-Crust Apple Pie

MAKES ONE 8-INCH PIE

QUICK PIE CRUST PASTRY
(Makes four 12-inch circles)

1 pound (4 sticks) unsalted butter
4 cups flour
1 tablespoon plus 1 teaspoon
  sugar
2 teaspoon salt
1/2 cup iced water

4 tart apples (McIntosh, Cortland, or Granny Smith), peeled, cored, and cut into thin wedges
1/2 cup sugar
1 teaspoon cinnamon
  Pinch of ground mace
  Pinch of grated nutmeg
2 tablespoons butter
  Confectioners' sugar
  Whipped cream

1. In the bowl of a food processor, combine the butter and dry ingredients. Process just until the mixture resembles coarse meal.

2. Add iced water bit by bit until the dough pulls away from the bowl and forms a solid mass. This process should take less than one minute.

3. Remove dough from bowl and knead once or twice on a floured surface. Divide dough into fourths, and roll each out to a 12-inch circle.

4. Fit one pastry circle into the pie plate and chill for 20 minutes (freeze the remaining three for future use). Fill the crust with apple slices. Sprinkle with sugar and spices, dot with butter, and fold the pastry edges over the apples.

5. Bake for 45 minutes in a preheated 375° oven, until the apple filling is bubbly and the crust is golden. Cool slightly and slide the pie out of the dish and onto a serving plate or board. Before serving sprinkle the crust with confectioners' sugar. Serve with a bowl of freshly whipped cream.

Sole with Black Butter and Capers

ONE OF MY FAVORITE RESTAU-
rants in New York was Le Mistral. It no longer exists, but during its period
of prominence Le Mistral presented a very excellent fillet of sole with what
I learned much later was called black butter. I like to top fish with this sauce,
which is simply slightly burned butter mixed with balsamic or sherry wine
vinegar and fried capers. Capers come in two sizes, and I prefer using the
smaller variety preserved in vinegar. To fry, simply drop well-drained capers
into hot oil, and they will open up and look like flowers.

A *tian* is actually a type of shallow earthenware casserole, usually oval.
Vegetables baked in the tian in overlapping layers with olive oil and fresh
herbs for flavor are delicious. This tian is composed of thinly sliced zucchini,
tomatoes, and potatoes. You can add eggs and create a frittata, or a light
custard and make a crustless quiche, but I prefer the vegetables all by themselves.

For dessert, an apple raspberry crumble baked in the oven along with
the casserole is an old-fashioned delight. In my family we love to eat it
warm, with softly whipped cream melting into the crumble topping. Each
June and July I freeze great quantities of raspberries for dishes such as these.
We pick the berries, taking care not to squash or bruise the fruit. The berries
are then put on cookie sheets and frozen, one layer at a time, in the coldest
part of the freezer. As soon as the berries are hard, they are packed into
rigid plastic freezing containers. This way we have whole, perfect berries
with no extra sugar or syrups. This same method works for blueberries,
blackberries, golden raspberries, and currants.

The beauty of fillet of sole is that it is always avail-able and can be quickly prepared in many differ-ent ways: broiled, baked, or sautéed, as here, with butter and capers. A fish-shaped tin candy mold contains black butter sauce, which is wonderful with the fish.

***

MENU
Salad of Escarole, Chicory, and Kirby Cucumbers
Sole with Black Butter and Capers
Tian of Zucchini, Tomatoes, and Potatoes
Apple Raspberry Crumble

Salad of Escarole, Chicory, and Kirby Cucumbers

SERVES 4

1/2 head curly chicory
1 head escarole
2 Kirby cucumbers, thinly sliced
1/3 cup light vegetable oil (such as safflower or sunflower)
3 tablespoons sherry wine vinegar
1 tablespoon brown sugar
1/4 cup yellow raisins

1. Wash and tear leaves of chicory and escarole. Dry well and put the leaves in a salad bowl. Arrange cucumber slices on top.

2. In a saucepan combine oil, vinegar, sugar, and raisins. Heat over medium flame until the sugar dissolves.

3. Pour dressing over the salad, toss well, and serve at once.

Sole with Black Butter and Capers

SERVES 4

1 1/2 pounds fillet of sole
Flour for dredging
3 tablespoons unsalted butter
2 tablespoons light vegetable oil
1/3 cup olive oil
1/3 cup tiny capers

BLACK BUTTER SAUCE

6 tablespoons (3/4 stick) unsalted butter
2 tablespoons balsamic or sherry vinegar

1. Cut the fillet of sole in half lengthwise. Dredge lightly with flour.

2. Heat butter and vegetable oil in a large skillet. Sauté the fish for 2 to 3 minutes on each side, or until firm and golden.

3. Remove the fish to a heated platter. Keep warm.

4. In a small skillet heat olive oil until very hot. Drop in the capers and fry until they puff open like flowers. Drain well and sprinkle over fish.

5. To make the sauce, melt the butter in a small skillet over medium heat until it becomes a nutty brown. Add the vinegar and stir well. Pour over the fish. Serve immediately.

Tian of Zucchini, Tomatoes, and Potatoes

SERVES 4

2 zucchini
2 tomatoes
2 baking potatoes
1/3 cup olive oil
10 leaves fresh basil
Salt and pepper to taste

1. Preheat the oven to 400°. Thinly slice the zucchini, tomatoes, and potatoes.

2. Arrange the vegetables in a lightly oiled shallow casserole dish, alternating the slices of vegetables. Coat them with olive oil and bake for 30 to 40 minutes, or until potatoes are tender.

3. Sprinkle basil and salt and pepper over vegetables. Serve hot.

Apple Raspberry Crumble

SERVES 4

3 Granny Smith apples
Juice of 1 lemon
1 10-ounce container frozen
   raspberries (or 1 pint fresh
   raspberries)
1 cup flour
1/2 cup sugar
1/2 cup (1 stick) unsalted butter
1/4 teaspoon nutmeg
Heavy cream

1. Preheat oven to 375°. Peel and core apples and cut each into 8 or 10 slices. Arrange them in a buttered shallow baking dish. Sprinkle lemon juice over them.

2. Drain the raspberries and reserve the juice for other use. Sprinkle the berries over the apples.

3. Mix flour and sugar in a bowl. Cut in the butter with your fingers until the mixture is crumbly. Add nutmeg and cover fruit with this mixture.

4. Bake for 25 minutes, or until the top is golden brown. Serve with heavy cream, softly whipped, if you wish.

Lamb Chops
with
Mint Butter

My 1930s Glenwood gas range in the new barn is the buffet for this dinner. The lamb chops and stuffed tomatoes are served directly from cast-iron pans, the french fried potatoes from flat Indian baskets. Individual medallions of mint butter add a flavorful touch to the lamb.

MENU
Lamb Chops with Mint Butter
French Fried Potatoes
Broiled Tomatoes
Sliced Mangoes, Indian Style

I VIVIDLY REMEMBER THE TEN-
derloin lamb chops that my Uncle Joe (Woije Joe) included for me in any purchase my mother made at his butcher shop in Jersey City. Mother would cook them my favorite way: in a black iron skillet with soft sweet butter and fresh mint. A few minutes under the broiler and the secret feast was all mine.

I've added a few other favorite things to this menu—shoestring potatoes deep fried in a cast-iron Japanese frying wok, broiled garden tomatoes flavored with parsley, and ripe mangoes for dessert.

Andy and I have always loved mangoes. There is something wonderful about taking a ripe, juicy mango right off the tree in some exotic place, like Haiti, and eating it immediately. Mangoes *are* messy to eat though. I never served them at more formal dinners until I learned in an Indian restaurant in Paris how to cut them so they can be eaten with a spoon (see recipe).

✺

Lamb Chops with Mint Butter
SERVES 3

2 tablespoons chopped fresh mint leaves, or 1 tablespoon dried
8 tablespoons (1 stick) unsalted butter, softened
1/4 teaspoon salt
Freshly ground pepper to taste
1 teaspoon lemon juice
3 loin lamb chops, 1 1/2 inches thick (or 6 thin rib lamb chops)

1. Preheat broiler.

2. In a food processor or a blender combine the mint, butter, salt, pepper, and lemon juice until smooth. Chill the mixture about 10 minutes, or just until firm enough to roll into a cylinder about 2 inches in diameter. Wrap in waxed paper and chill another 10 minutes. Slice into medallions.

3. With a sharp knife score lamb chops on both sides. Coat them with the mint butter and let them stand for 30 to 40 minutes at room temperature.

4. Broil the chops for 8 to 10 minutes, turning at least twice. Serve directly from the broiler onto individual plates.

French Fried Potatoes

SERVES 3

> 3 *large baking potatoes*
> *Olive oil for deep frying (about 2*
> *inches deep in a heavy pan)*
> *Coarse salt*

1. Peel the potatoes and slice lengthwise, 1/4 inch thick, and cut each slice into sticks 1/4 inch wide. Soak in salted water for 30 minutes.

2. Drain the potatoes and dry thoroughly. Heat oil to about 385°. Spoon the potatoes into the hot oil and gently move them about with a slotted spoon. Fry until crisp and golden brown. Remove them and drain on a rack or paper towels. Serve immediately with a sprinkling of salt.

❧

Broiled Tomatoes

SERVES 3

> 2 *tablespoons (1/4 stick) unsalted*
> *butter*
> 1/4 *cup fresh bread crumbs*
> 2 *tablespoons chopped parsley*
> 3 *ripe tomatoes*
> *Salt and pepper to taste*

1. Preheat broiler.

2. In a small skillet melt butter over medium high heat and sauté bread crumbs until golden. Remove from the heat and mix with the parsley. Season to taste with salt and pepper.

3. Cut about 1/2 inch off the top of each tomato and a small sliver off the bottom, just enough to allow them to stand upright. Sprinkle lightly with salt.

4. Top each tomato with a generous tablespoon of the bread-crumb mixture and arrange the tomatoes on a baking sheet. Broil for 4 to 5 minutes. The tomatoes should be firm but warm and the topping golden brown. Serve immediately.

❧

Sliced Mangoes, Indian Style

SERVES 4

Take 2 large ripe mangoes and, using a sharp stainless steel knife, slice each lengthwise into 2 pieces, avoiding the elongated pit in the center. Discard the pit. Score the flesh of each half, making a fine crisscross pattern. Do not cut through the skin. Turn each mango half inside out and serve on a dessert plate with a wedge of lime.

A single pork chop makes an impressive display on a late-nineteenth-century Majolica plate (opposite). A small bouquet of Dutch iris in a glass is the only adornment needed for the table. Left: amethyst dessert glasses and plates hold the ice cream with chocolate ganache topping. I like to serve heart-shaped cut-out cookies with the dessert.

Pork Chops with Fennel

❦

MENU
**Watercress Salad with Julienned Pears and Blue Cheese
Pork Chops with Fennel
Turnips Dauphinoise
Vanilla Ice Cream with Hot Chocolate Ganache**

*C*HIS IS ANOTHER OF MY FAV-
orite ways to cook pork chops. The thick-cut chops (loin chops make a very
nice presentation) are sautéed in olive oil with fennel leaves until done; then
the pan is deglazed with fresh orange juice. The chops are always succulent,
never dry and tough, when cooked this way. While the chops are sautéing,
a dish of thinly sliced white turnips is baked in the oven with a covering of
buttery cream flavored with thyme. Generally potatoes are scalloped like
this, but the turnips are unusual and very good.

Dessert is vanilla ice cream with chocolate ganache—semisweet chocolate of very good quality melted in hot heavy cream. Ganache is the basis
for chocolate truffles: the hardened chocolate-cream mixture can be formed
into small balls and rolled in cocoa, ground nuts, or powdered sugar.

❧

Watercress Salad with Julienned Pears and Blue Cheese

SERVES 4

*Allow a small handful of
     watercress per person, with
     stems removed*
2 *ripe Comice or Packham pears,
     cored and sliced*
1/2 *cup crumbled Blue cheese*

RASPBERRY VINAIGRETTE
(Makes 1 cup)

1/4 *cup raspberry vinegar*
2/3 *cup olive oil*
     Salt and pepper to taste

1. Arrange some of the watercress, pears, and cheese on individual serving plates.

2. Combine ingredients for the vinaigrette in a mixing bowl and pour
over the salads. Serve immediately.

Note: If you slice the pears 30 minutes or more before serving, toss the slices
in lemon juice to prevent darkening.

❧

Pork Chops with Fennel

SERVES 4

4 *tablespoons olive oil*
4 *loin pork chops (1 1/2 inches
     thick)*
     Salt and pepper to taste
1/2 *cup chopped fennel leaves*
     Juice of 2 oranges

1. In a large heavy skillet heat the oil and sauté the pork chops over medium-high heat for 13 to 15 minutes, turning twice.

2. Sprinkle with salt and pepper and fennel during the last 5 minutes of cooking. Remove chops from the skillet and keep warm.

3. Deglaze the skillet with the orange juice and bring to a boil. Reduce the liquid by a fourth and spoon over the chops. Serve immediately.

Turnips Dauphinoise

SERVES 4

> **3 tablespoons unsalted butter**
> **2 pounds small white turnips,**
>   **peeled and thinly sliced**
> **1 1/4 cups heavy cream, heated**
> **Fresh thyme leaves to taste**
> **Salt and pepper to taste**

1. Preheat oven to 350°. Butter a shallow earthenware casserole dish.

2. Arrange the turnip slices in the casserole and dot with butter. Pour the hot cream over the turnips. Sprinkle with thyme and salt and pepper.

3. Cook for 45 minutes, or until the turnips are tender and the cream has thickened.

Vanilla Ice Cream with Hot Chocolate Ganache

SERVES 4

> **3/4 pound semisweet chocolate**
> **3/4 cup heavy cream**
> **1 pint vanilla ice cream**

1. Chop the chocolate into chip-size pieces and put in a medium-size heatproof bowl.

2. Bring the cream to a full boil in a small saucepan. Pour immediately over the chocolate and stir until the chocolate is melted and smooth. (You can add a tablespoon of your favorite liqueur to the chocolate if you desire.)

3. Spoon warm mixture over ice cream. Serve.

Note: If the ganache hardens, put the bowl over simmering water and melt the chocolate, stirring occasionally. Do not overheat or the chocolate will separate and become grainy.

Smoked Turkey
and Stilton Sandwiches

*L*AST YEAR MY BROTHER GEORGE built us a smokehouse. It's a small affair, beautifully constructed from old pine, cedar shingles, and old brick. The smoking fire is contained in a pit in the brick floor, and meats and fish can be smoked on racks above and to the sides of the fire, or hanging on hooks from the rafters. We make the fires from hardwoods—cuttings from the fruit trees, hurricane-felled hickory trees—and charcoal. Often we add mesquite wood from the Southwest (which you can buy in bags from gourmet-food catalogs) for an intense, aromatic flavor. Since its construction, we have smoked fillets of beef, oysters, chickens, ducks, pheasants, shrimp, trout, and turkeys (wild and domestic). The smoked turkeys are especially delicious, and we use lots of them for hors d'oeuvre and buffet parties. The sandwiches in this menu are made of smoked turkey and Stilton cheese, a combination I adore. As pictured, they can be made on toasted bread and served with lettuce, or broiled for a few minutes to just melt the cheese.

The ginger pear soup is an invention of one of my cooks, Lisa Krieger. It reminds me of a wonderful thin pear sauce, subtly flavored with fresh ginger and spices.

The three-cabbage slaw is colorful, crunchy, and healthy; and the dressing is unusual, including scallion, cornichons, and celery seeds.

The simple walnut pound cake is just that. It's very easy to make and keeps well for days.

The simplicity of sandwich preparation means you can spend more time making interesting side dishes, like this spicy ginger pear soup and colorful three-cabbage slaw served in pinkware bowls from a rectangular copper tray. The smoked turkey sandwiches are on an Art Nouveau Limoges platter.

❧

MENU
Ginger Pear Soup
Three-Cabbage Slaw
Smoked Turkey and Stilton Sandwiches
Simple Walnut Pound Cake

Ginger Pear Soup

SERVES 4

6 ripe pears (Packham, Comice, or Bartlett), peeled and cored
3 1/2 cups water
1/4 cup sugar (or to taste)
1 vanilla bean
1 cinnamon stick
4 whole cloves
1 1/2-inch-thick slice fresh ginger
Powdered ginger to taste

1. Poach the pears in the water and sugar along with the vanilla bean, cinnamon stick, cloves, and ginger slice for approximately 35 to 40 minutes. When pears are soft, drain and reserve liquid. Discard vanilla, cinnamon, and cloves.

2. Purée the pears and ginger slice in a food processor until smooth. Pour mixture back into the saucepan.

3. Add two cups of the poaching liquid, or just enough to get a souplike consistency. Heat over medium-low flame. Sprinkle with powdered ginger and serve.

Three-Cabbage Slaw

SERVES 4

Allow 1 large handful of a combination of red cabbage, green cabbage, and bok choy (Chinese cabbage) per person

DRESSING (Makes 1 cup)

1 scallion, cut into 1/2-inch pieces
2 cornichons
2 egg yolks
1 teaspoon celery seeds
1 tablespoon rice vinegar
1 tablespoon Dijon mustard
1 teaspoon salt
3/4 cup vegetable oil
Salt and pepper to taste

1. With a sharp knife, shred the cabbages and put them in a salad bowl.

2. To make the dressing, chop the scallion and cornichons in a blender. Add the egg yolks, celery seeds, vinegar, mustard, and salt, and blend well.

3. With the blender running, add the oil, drop by drop, to make a thick mayonnaise. Toss the dressing with the shredded cabbages. Season with salt and pepper, if necessary, and chill until ready to serve.

Smoked Turkey and Stilton Sandwiches

SERVES 4

1/2 pound smoked turkey, thinly
    sliced
1/2 pound Stilton cheese, thinly
    sliced
    Lettuce or sprigs of watercress
8 slices whole-wheat French
    bread, lightly toasted and
    buttered
    Prepared mustard

Arrange the turkey, Stilton, and greens on top of the bread. Serve with your favorite mustard.

Simple Walnut Pound Cake

MAKES 1 LOAF OR ONE 9-INCH ROUND CAKE

1/2 pound (2 sticks) unsalted butter
1 tablespoon almond paste
2/3 cup brown sugar
1/2 teaspoon allspice
3 eggs, separated
1 1/2 cups all-purpose flour
1 1/2 teaspoons baking soda
    Pinch of salt
1 cup sour cream
1 teaspoon vanilla extract
1/4 cup white sugar
1 cup crushed walnuts

1. Preheat oven to 350°. Butter and flour a baking pan. Set aside.

2. Cream the butter, almond paste, brown sugar, and allspice until light and fluffy. Add the egg yolks and beat until well incorporated.

3. In a separate bowl sift together the flour, baking soda, and salt, and stir into the butter, alternating with the sour cream.

4. Beat the egg whites with the vanilla to a soft peak. Add the white sugar, a little at a time, and beat to a stiff peak.

5. Stir a third of the egg whites into the batter and mix in the walnuts. Fold the batter into the remaining egg whites, a little at a time.

6. Pour the batter into the prepared pan and bake for 30 to 40 minutes, or until the edges of the cake pull away slightly from the pan. A toothpick inserted in the center should come out clean. Cool for several minutes on a rack before unmolding.

Clay and earthenware casseroles, which are used both for cooking and serving, emphasize the informality of this hearty meal. Linen dishtowels also have a dual purpose: they are both potholders and napkins.

Crusty Mustard Chicken

❧

MENU
Crusty Mustard Chicken
Tian of Potatoes, Zucchini, Eggplant, and Whole Garlic
Brussels Sprouts with Cream
Cranberry Kuchen

This luscious cranberry kuchen is one of my family's favorite desserts. We love to eat it hot from the oven with cream and a sprinkling of sugar.

W*HEN WE CREATED PICNIC BOX* suppers for the Stratford Shakespeare Theatre in 1977 and 1978 this crusty mustard chicken was by far the most popular. It can be made for six persons or for sixty, and the result will be equally good. The whole cooking process is done under a preheated broiler. The chicken can be reheated in a 375° oven if you wish to serve it some time after preparation; it is also delicious warm, at room temperature, or cold.

A tian of thinly sliced eggplant, potatoes, and zucchini accompanies the chicken. A whole head of garlic sits in the middle of this casserole and is roasted along with the other vegetables. I love to cook garlic this way. The cloves become soft and tender, and the strong flavor disappears, leaving a gentle, sweet taste.

The Brussels sprouts, too, are cooked in a new way. The little sprouts are cooked whole, and then the leaves are peeled off one by one and added to hot cream seasoned with thyme.

Crusty Mustard Chicken

SERVES 4 TO 6

8 tablespoons (1 stick) unsalted
butter
2 tablespoons vegetable oil
6 tablespoons Dijon mustard
3 tablespoons minced shallots
2 tablespoons fresh thyme leaves
1 teaspoon freshly ground black
pepper
1/2 teaspoon crushed red pepper
2 2½-pound broiler chickens cut
into 8 pieces each
4 cups fresh white bread crumbs

1. Preheat broiler. Broil chicken for 3 minutes on each side and remove.

2. Melt the butter in the oil over low heat. Set aside.

3. In a mixing bowl combine the mustard, shallots, thyme, black pepper, and red pepper. Stir in half the butter and oil mixture and blend thoroughly.

4. Brush the chicken pieces with the mustard mixture and roll them in the bread crumbs to coat completely. Dab them with the remaining melted butter and oil.

5. Arrange the pieces on a broiler pan and cook under a medium-hot broiler for 10 to 12 minutes, turning them two or three times. The chicken is done when the juices run clear when it is pricked with a knife. If the chicken pieces are getting too brown, finish them in a 550° oven.

Tian of Potatoes, Zucchini, Eggplant, and Whole Garlic

SERVES 4 TO 6

3 baking potatoes, peeled
3 long, pale purple Japanese
eggplants
3 zucchini
1 head garlic, unpeeled
Salt and pepper to taste
1/2 cup olive oil
5 to 6 sprigs rosemary

1. Preheat oven to 400°. Thinly slice potatoes, eggplants, and zucchini.

2. Arrange vegetables in a shallow baking dish, alternating each.

3. Put the garlic in the center of the dish. Sprinkle with salt and pepper and pour the oil over the vegetables.

4. Arrange the rosemary sprigs on top of the vegetables and bake for 30 to 40 minutes, or until the potatoes are tender. Pour off excess oil and serve immediately.

❧

Brussels Sprouts with Cream

SERVES 4 TO 6

> 1 quart Brussels sprouts
> 1/2 cup heavy cream
> 2 to 3 sprigs fresh thyme
> Salt and pepper to taste

1. Trim and wash the Brussels sprouts. Cook them in a large kettle of lightly salted boiling water until tender, 10 to 12 minutes. Drain and cool under cold running water. Remove leaves from each Brussels sprout and set aside.

2. Bring the cream to a boil. Add the thyme and Brussels sprout leaves. Season with salt and pepper and serve hot.

❧

Cranberry Kuchen

MAKES ONE 8-INCH ROUND CAKE

TOPPING

1/2 pound fresh cranberries
1/2 cup sugar
1/4 cup water
Juice of 1 orange

BATTER

2/3 cup (1 1/3 sticks) unsalted
   butter, at room temperature
1/2 cup sugar
2 eggs
1 1/2 cups flour
1 1/2 teaspoons baking powder
1/2 cup milk
2 tablespoons sour cream
Grated rind of 1 orange
Fresh nutmeg to taste

1. Preheat oven to 350°. Butter and flour an 8-inch round baking pan.

2. In a small saucepan combine all the ingredients for the topping. Bring to a boil, reduce heat, and cook until the cranberries are soft, about 10 minutes. Set aside.

3. In a mixing bowl cream the butter and sugar with an electric mixer or a wooden spoon. Add the eggs, one at a time, stirring well to incorporate.

4. Sift together the flour and the baking powder. Stir the flour into the butter mixture, a little at a time, alternating with milk and sour cream. Stir in the orange rind and nutmeg.

5. Pour the batter into the prepared pan and top with the cranberry mixture. Bake for about 40 minutes, or until golden brown.

Mussels with Pesto

ONE SEPTEMBER LONG AGO ANDY and I spent a weekend on a small island off the coast of Jamestown, Rhode Island. The entire island appeared to be made of mussels, which varied in size from tiny to large. We simply had to pull clumps of mussels from the rocks and throw them into huge kettles with white wine and herbs for an almost instantaneous dinner of *moules marinières*. The mussels were unbelievably clean—no scrubbing was required—and sweet and plump as could be. The following menu offers steamed mussels with a pesto sauce, a basil and olive oil mixture that goes very well with shellfish and pasta. The fettuccine is served with a fresh sauce, a concasse, made from shallots and crushed tomatoes.

Roasted red peppers are an especially wonderful vegetable. To roast, put the whole pepper on a fork and hold it directly over flames on a grill or over a gas flame. When the skin is completely black, put in a brown paper bag to "sweat." After 5 minutes the skin rubs off quite easily. The peppers can then be seeded, cut into pieces, and served with olive oil and garlic. For an even more colorful salad, roast red, green, and yellow bell peppers and arrange them in overlapping layers. The roasted peppers are excellent as a first course or as a salad course. They have lots of other uses as well—they make wonderful red pepper soup and are a colorful addition to pasta.

Black Colombian pottery dishes accentuate the deep, rich colors of this meal of steamed mussels and roasted red peppers sprinkled with minced garlic.

MENU
Roasted Red Peppers
Mussels with Pesto
Fettuccine with Tomato Concasse
Espresso Sorbet

Roasted Red Peppers

SERVES 6

6 large red bell peppers (or yellow
   peppers, or a combination of
   the two)
1/2 cup olive oil
2 cloves garlic, minced
   Salt and pepper to taste

1. Roast the peppers on all sides over an open gas flame until the skins are black. (You can grill or broil them instead.)

2. Put the peppers in a large paper bag for 5 minutes to "sweat" them. Remove from the bag and rub off the pepper skins with your fingers.

3. Seed the peppers and cut them lengthwise into quarters.

4. Put peppers on a serving platter and toss with olive oil, garlic, and salt and pepper.

Mussels with Pesto

SERVES 6

1/2 cup water
1/2 cup Dubonnet Blanc (or dry
   vermouth)
1 medium-size bunch fresh basil
   leaves
48 mussels, beards removed and
   well scrubbed

PESTO SAUCE

4 cloves garlic, peeled
1/2 cup pine nuts
1 teaspoon coarse salt
1/2 teaspoon freshly ground pepper
3 to 4 cups fresh basil leaves
1/4 pound fresh Parmesan cheese,
   grated
1/4 pound fresh Romano cheese,
   grated
1 1/2 to 2 cups olive oil

1. In a saucepan large enough to hold a steamer, combine the water and Dubonnet.

2. Line the steamer with the basil leaves and put the mussels on top.

3. Cover, bring liquid to a boil, and steam mussels until opened, 4 to 6 minutes. Do not overcook or the mussels will shrink.

4. Remove half of each mussel shell, and put the other half (with mussel) on a baking sheet. Set aside.

5. To make the pesto, blend the garlic, pine nuts, salt, pepper, basil, both cheeses, and 1/2 cup of the oil in a food processor. With the machine running, add remaining oil in a slow, steady stream until the mixture is smooth and creamy.

6. Spoon a small amount of pesto on top of each mussel. Put them under the broiler and cook until glazed. Serve hot.

Fettuccine with Tomato Concasse

SERVES 6

> 2 tablespoons (1/4 stick) unsalted butter
> 2 shallots, minced
> 2 tablespoons olive oil
> 6 tomatoes, peeled and seeded
>   Salt and pepper to taste
> 1 1/2 pounds egg fettuccine

1. In a skillet melt the butter over medium heat and sauté the shallots until soft. Add the olive oil and tomatoes, season lightly with salt and pepper, and remove from the heat.

2. Cook the fettuccine in a large pot of lightly salted boiling water until tender. Drain and put in a serving bowl. Toss with the tomato concasse and serve.

Espresso Sorbet

MAKES 1 QUART (IN AN ICE-CREAM MACHINE)

> 1/2 cup espresso beans, finely ground
> 2 3/4 cups water
> 1 vanilla bean
> 3/4 cup sugar

1. Make espresso coffee with the ground beans and 2 cups water. Add the vanilla bean and cool in the refrigerator.

2. Combine 3/4 cup water with the sugar in a saucepan. Bring to a boil, remove from the heat, and combine with the coffee. Chill in the refrigerator.

3. Discard the vanilla bean and freeze according to the ice cream maker's instructions.

Roast Pheasant

$\mathcal{M}$*ANY OF MY FRIENDS PARTICI-*
pate in a sport of which I'm not personally very fond, bird shooting. They often return home laden with the bounty of the hunt and leave a few pheasant or quail for Andy and me. I learned from my grandmother how to clean and pluck all kinds of birds, and I did it often, so it does not bother me. I'm very careful not to break the skin and to pluck very clean so that the final product looks almost store-bought.

We've developed many recipes for the preparation of wild game. I prefer it roasted, grilled, or quickly sautéed. This menu offers a recipe for simple roast pheasant, lightly flavored with garlic and thyme or rosemary. Another good way to cook pheasant is to sauté it in butter with rosemary, garlic, and pepper and to then lightly braise it with dry white wine. Before roasting or sautéing, it is lovely to marinate the birds in wine or berry juice, possibly with juniper berries, herbs, shallots and berries such as currants, blackberries, or blueberries.

The first course is preceded by a thick soup of broccoli, and a simple salad of lima beans and radicchio is served with the pheasant. For dessert, ice cream with my friend Ruth's homemade candied ginger butterscotch sauce is perfect.

A Japanese silk obi is the table covering for this elegant autumn supper. The soup is served in individual cups of Stickware, very old and very rare. The radicchio not only tastes delicious but it also makes a wonderful "bowl" for the lima bean salad.

MENU
Broccoli Soup
Roast Pheasant
Lima Bean and Radicchio Salad
Ice Cream with Homemade Candied
Ginger Butterscotch Sauce

Broccoli Soup

> 6 tablespoons (3/4 stick) unsalted butter
> 1 leek, minced
> 1 carrot, minced
> 2 cloves garlic, minced
> 4 cups chicken stock
> 1 head broccoli, cut into small flowerets
> 1 cup heavy cream
> 1 pinch cayenne pepper
> 1 teaspoon celery seed

1. In a pot melt the butter over medium heat. Add the leek, carrot, and garlic. Cook until they are tender, about 5 minutes, making sure they do not brown.

2. Add the stock. Bring to a simmer, and add broccoli. Cook for 8 to 10 minutes, or until broccoli is tender.

3. Pour the soup into a food processor and process until the vegetables are finely chopped but not puréed. Pour soup back into the pot. Stir in the cream, cayenne pepper, and celery seed. Reheat before serving.

Roast Pheasant

SERVES 4

> 2 2-pound pheasants
> Salt and pepper to taste
> 1 head garlic
> 4 sprigs fresh thyme
> 4 slices bacon
> 1/2 cup (1 stick) unsalted butter, melted

1. Preheat the oven to 375°. Rub the cavity of the pheasants with salt and pepper. Place half of the garlic and 2 sprigs thyme in each of them.

2. Wrap 2 slices of bacon around each pheasant breast. Truss them with a string and put in a baking dish.

3. Cook the pheasants for 45 to 60 minutes, basting often with melted butter. Fifteen minutes before they are done, remove the bacon strips and baste the breasts to brown them. The pheasants should not be overcooked. They are usually served when the flesh is pink. To test, prick the thickest part of the thigh. When the juices run pinkish to clear, they are done.

Lima Bean and Radicchio Salad

SERVES 3 TO 4

1 package frozen lima beans or 1
  cup fresh beans
1 or 2 small heads radicchio
  lettuce

VINAIGRETTE (Makes 1/2 cup)

3 tablespoons champagne or white
  wine vinegar
2 tablespoons olive oil
1/4 cup vegetable oil (safflower or
  soy)
Pinch of sugar
Salt and pepper to taste

1. In a small pot bring lightly salted water to a boil. Add lima beans and cook until tender. Drain. Plunge them into ice-cold water to chill. Drain well.

2. Separate and tear the radicchio leaves. Arrange them on individual plates with a tablespoon or two of lima beans.

3. In a small mixing bowl combine all the ingredients for the vinaigrette. Stir well and spoon the vinaigrette over each serving.

Ice Cream with Homemade Candied Ginger Butterscotch Sauce

MAKES 1 1/2 CUPS

1 cup sugar
1/2 cup water
1 1/2 cups heavy cream, at room
  temperature
3 tablespoons butter
1 to 2 tablespoons chopped
  candied ginger, according to
  taste

1. Combine sugar and water in a saucepan. Cook over high heat for about 5 to 10 minutes, or until mixture is light golden brown. Remove from the heat.

2. Add the cream and stir until smooth. Add the butter, a teaspoon at a time. Blend well.

3. Add the candied ginger, stir well, and spoon over ice cream.

Sea Scallops Sautéed
with Scallions

*I*N 1962, WHEN I VISITED
Paris for the first time, I discovered fresh sea scallops *en coquille* in a small
restaurant behind the Luxembourg Gardens. The unusual thing about those
scallops was that the orange roe was still attached. It was extraordinarily
delicious, and ever since I have tried to find such scallops in the United
States. Sometimes on Martha's Vineyard, in autumn, one can harvest scallops and remove them from their shells with the roe. Several importers are
now selling scallops this way. In any event, for this dish be sure to use
scallops that are extremely fresh. They should smell sweet and very mild.

Spaghetti is served with an uncooked tomato sauce as a side dish. The
tomatoes can be of the plum variety, which have very few seeds, or of a
larger type, in which case they should be peeled and seeded. Use only very
red, ripe tomatoes when making this sauce.

Late summer and early fall is the time when peaches are harvested.
Sliced and served with brown sugar and Cognac, ripe peaches are a wonderful dessert for this menu.

*The bottom half of a
Moroccan clay tagine is
an excellent serving dish
for any food with a sauce.*

MENU
Sea Scallops Sautéed with Scallions
Spaghetti with Uncooked Tomato Sauce
Sautéed Green Beans
Whole-Wheat Italian Bread with Herb Butter
Sliced Peaches with Brown Sugar and Cognac

Sea Scallops Sautéed with Scallions

SERVES 4

1/2 cup flour
1/2 teaspoon salt
Freshly ground pepper to taste
1 1/2 pounds sea scallops, cut in half
4 tablespoons (1/2 stick) unsalted butter
1/4 cup vegetable oil
1 small bunch scallions, sliced
1/3 cup dry white wine
3 tablespoons chopped fresh chervil or parsley
Lemon wedges

1. On a plate combine flour, salt, and pepper. Dredge the scallops in it.

2. In a large heavy skillet heat the butter and oil and sauté the scallops very quickly until golden brown, about 4 minutes. Remove scallops with a slotted spoon and put on a warmed serving dish. Sauté the scallions in the same skillet over medium-high heat for 5 minutes. They should not brown. Remove with a slotted spoon and sprinkle over the scallops. Keep warm.

3. Pour off the excess oil from the pan. Add white wine and deglaze the pan over high heat until the wine is reduced by half. Pour sauce over the scallops, sprinkle with fresh herbs, and serve immediately with lemon.

Spaghetti with Uncooked Tomato Sauce

SERVES 4

1 pound spaghetti (fresh if possible)
1/2 cup grated Parmesan cheese

SAUCE

2 pounds very ripe tomatoes
1 small onion, minced
1 clove garlic, minced
1/2 cup fresh basil, chopped
1/2 cup olive oil
Salt and freshly ground pepper to taste

1. Drop the tomatoes into 4 quarts boiling water. Remove after 1 minute. When they are cool enough to handle, peel, seed, and coarsely chop them.

2. In a bowl mix the chopped tomatoes with the onion, garlic, basil, oil, and salt and pepper. Let sit at room temperature for 1 hour before serving.

3. Cook the pasta in a large pot of boiling salted water until *al dente*. Drain.

4. In a large bowl toss the pasta with the tomato sauce and serve immediately with Parmesan cheese.

Sautéed Green Beans

SERVES 4

> 1 pound string beans
> 2 tablespoons (1/4 stick) unsalted butter
> Salt and pepper to taste

1. Cook the beans in lightly salted boiling water for 3 to 4 minutes. Transfer them into ice water to cool. Drain again.

2. When ready to serve, melt the butter in a sauté pan and cook the beans quickly to heat them. Season to taste and serve.

Note: You can also cook the beans for 3 to 4 minutes in the boiling water, drain, and serve immediately, dotted with butter.

Whole-Wheat Italian Bread with Herb Butter

SERVES 4

1 loaf whole-wheat Italian bread

HERB BUTTER (Makes 1 pound)

> 4 tablespoons finely chopped parsley
> 2 tablespoons finely chopped dill, chervil, or tarragon
> 1 pound (4 sticks) unsalted butter, at room temperature

1. To make the herb butter, chop all herbs in a food processor, add softened butter, and mix together. Pack into butter molds or crocks. The butter will keep up to 2 days in the refrigerator, or can be frozen for future use.

2. Cut the bread lengthwise into halves and spread each half with softened herb butter. Put them on a baking sheet and toast in the oven until crispy. Slice and serve immediately.

Sliced Peaches with Brown Sugar and Cognac

SERVES 4

> 4 large freestone peaches
> 4 tablespoons brown sugar
> 2 tablespoons Cognac
> Crème fraîche (optional)

1. Slice the peaches and remove the pits.

2. Arrange the slices on dessert plates. Sprinkle with sugar and Cognac. Serve immediately with a bowl of crème fraîche.

Grilled Breast of Duck

LAST FALL WE HAD SEVERAL guests to dinner and served them this menu, which was exciting to prepare because it was so different. Frozen whole breasts of duck were thawed and marinated in black currant juice overnight in the refrigerator.* Then we built a fire in our old hibachi, right in the kitchen fireplace, and grilled the duck breasts until the skin was very black and the flesh was cooked but pink. The breast meat was carved into thin slices and served with crispy, golden brown fried potato chips. Be sure you make lots of these chips, for they will be consumed at a rapid rate. Beet purée and an autumnal salad are good accompaniments to the dinner. The honey mustard vinaigrette makes the chicory taste less bitter.

You can buy canned black currants in syrup from the Krakus Company. I use the black currants for sorbet and for dessert sauces. Black currants are difficult to locate in the U.S. and are imported only at one time of the year, usually January, from New Zealand. At that time you could freeze or can your own juice and berries, but it is much more economical to buy commercially prepared berries. For dessert serve a selection of apples and cheeses according to your preference.

* Frozen duck breasts are becoming increasingly available in supermarkets all over the country. They are wonderful to have on hand for quick cooking, as are whole frozen chicken and turkey breasts.

Every time I go to a tag sale I search for odd pieces of this brown Stangl spatterware, which is no longer being manufactured. I think it makes an especially beautiful table. The duck in this menu should be accompanied by a hearty Burgundy wine.

❧

MENU
Grilled Breast of Duck
Chicory Salad
Potato Slices Fried in Olive Oil
Purée of Beets
Apples and Cheese

Grilled Breast of Duck

SERVES 2

1 cup black currant juice or syrup
    from any canned fruit (pears,
    peaches, etc.)
1/2 cup red wine
4 to 6 sprigs fresh thyme
1 whole duck breast, bones in and
    skin on, fresh or frozen

1. Combine juice, wine, and thyme. Marinate the duck breast in this mixture for at least 30 minutes, or overnight in the refrigerator if the duck is frozen.

2. To cook the duck, put the breast on a hot charcoal fire or under a preheated broiler and grill for about 7 to 9 minutes on each side. (Be careful, because the fat might cause the fire to flame.) The skin of the duck should blacken but the meat should be pink.

3. Carve the meat from the bone in thin slices and serve.

❧

Chicory Salad

SERVES 2

1 medium head chicory (about 3/4
    pound)

HONEY MUSTARD VINAIGRETTE
(Makes 1 cup)

1/2 cup vegetable oil
1/4 cup olive oil
3 tablespoons champagne or white
    wine vinegar
1 tablespoon whole-grain mustard
1 tablespoon honey
    Salt and pepper to taste

1. Wash and tear the leaves of chicory. Arrange them in a salad bowl.

2. Combine all the ingredients for the vinaigrette. Pour over the lettuce and toss well.

Purée of Beets

SERVES 2

1 small bunch beets (4 to 6)
1 tablespoon cider vinegar
2 tablespoons heavy cream or
crème fraîche (see page 17)
Zest of 1 orange
Salt and pepper to taste

1. Put the beets in cold water, bring to a boil, reduce heat, and cook over medium flame until tender, about 25 to 30 minutes.

2. Peel the beets and purée in a food processor. Stir in vinegar, cream, orange zest, and salt and pepper. Serve warm.

Potato Slices Fried in Olive Oil

SERVES 2

2 cups light olive oil
2 to 3 baking potatoes, peeled and
thinly sliced
Kosher salt and pepper to taste

1. Heat the oil in a cast-iron pan until very hot.

2. Add the potato slices (about 1 potato at a time) and fry, stirring gently with a wooden spoon or wire strainer, until a rich golden brown. Drain on paper towel, season with salt and pepper, and serve immediately.

Apples and Cheese

This is a most simple dessert. Choose extra-fine apples (Granny Smith, Golden Delicious, Cortland, and Macoun are good with cheese), and provide either one large cheese—a perfectly ripe Camembert or Explorateur, or a small selection of little goat cheeses. A wedge of Vermont Cheddar would also be a nice offering.

The easy yet spectacular chocolate mousse tart (opposite) *can be topped with chocolate curls, which can be made ahead and kept in the freezer for several weeks. Melt semisweet chocolate in a double boiler over hot water, spread on a sturdy cookie sheet, and refrigerate until slightly hardened, about 15 minutes. With a metal pastry scraper at a 45-degree angle, scrape to produce curls. If the chocolate sticks to the scraper, it is not firm enough and should be refrigerated further; if it splinters, it is too hard.*

Pan-Fried Fillet of Beef

*C*HE MOST COMPLICATED DISH in this menu is a very simple Pommes Anna—thinly sliced potatoes cooked in a shallow pan in clarified butter until tender and crispy. The thick fillets of beef are cut from the whole fillet and can be cooked quickly to order. Baby carrots are braised until tender. Watercress, which we are more accustomed to eating in salads, is delicious when lightly sautéed in butter with a bit of garlic and balsamic vinegar.

Dessert for this menu is an elegant chocolate mousse tart devised by Jane Stacey, my pastry chef. You will need to prepare the tart shell well ahead—pastry shells can be kept frozen for several months if well wrapped. The mousse must be made the day you wish to serve the tart.

❦

MENU
Pan-Fried Fillet of Beef
Pommes Anna
Braised Whole Young Carrots
Sautéed Watercress
Jane's Chocolate Mousse Tart

Pan-Fried Fillet of Beef

SERVES 2

2 2-inch-thick fillets (tournedos)
2 tablespoons (1/4 stick) unsalted butter
Salt and freshly ground black pepper to taste
2 teaspoons herb butter (optional)

1. If necessary, tie a string around the fillets to maintain their shape.

2. Heat the butter over high heat in a heavy iron skillet or enameled frypan. Quickly sauté the meat to sear the outside. Reduce heat to medium high and continue cooking until meat is done to taste—6 to 10 minutes for rare fillets.

3. Put tournedos on warm dinner plates. Sprinkle each with salt and pepper, and a teaspoon of herb butter if desired.

Pommes Anna

SERVES 2

3 large baking potatoes, peeled and thinly sliced
8 tablespoons (1 stick) clarified unsalted butter
1 teaspoon salt

1. Preheat oven to 400°.

2. Pour 2 tablespoons of the clarified butter into an iron skillet or a copper Pommes Anna pan. Arrange potato slices in the pan in concentric circles, overlapping the slices, and dribble each layer with butter and sprinkle with salt. Heat the pan on top of the stove until the butter bubbles.

3. Bake in the oven until the potatoes are golden brown and soft, approximately 20 minutes. Press the potatoes with a pot lid during the baking once or twice to keep them flat.

4. Remove from the oven and pour off excess butter. Put a serving dish on top of the pan and flip the two as you would to unmold a cake. Serve.

Braised Whole Young Carrots

SERVES 2

In a medium saucepan, put 8 to 10 small peeled carrots, a pinch of sugar, 1 tablespoon unsalted butter, and water to cover. Bring to a boil and cook until the carrots are tender, 8 to 12 minutes. Drain, season to taste with salt and pepper, and serve.

Sautéed Watercress

SERVES 2

Melt 2 tablespoons unsalted butter in a large frypan. Add a peeled and sliced garlic clove and cook over medium-high heat for 1 minute. Toss in 1 bunch of watercress and cook just until it wilts. Pour in 1 tablespoon balsamic vinegar, heat thoroughly, and serve.

❧

Jane's Chocolate Mousse Tart

MAKES ONE 8-INCH TART

TART SHELL

1 1/4 cups flour
2 tablespoons sugar
Dash of salt
1/2 cup (1 stick) unsalted butter, cold and cut into small pieces
1 egg, slightly beaten
3/4 cup ground walnuts (or ground roasted hazelnuts, almonds, pistachios, or Brazil nuts)
1 teaspoon vanilla extract or 1/2 teaspoon almond extract

MOUSSE

8 ounces semisweet chocolate
4 ounces unsweetened chocolate
3/4 cup unsalted butter
5 eggs, separated
3 tablespoons liqueur (Cognac, rum, kirsch, Kahlua, or your favorite)
Pinch of cream of tartar
2 tablespoons to 1/4 cup sugar, to taste
1 cup heavy cream
Chocolate curls (optional)

1. To make the tart shell, combine flour, sugar, and salt. Cut butter into the flour until mixture is crumbly. Add the egg and mix until well combined. Stir in the nuts and vanilla. Mix by hand or in an electric mixer at low speed until the dough forms a ball.

2. Press or roll the dough firmly into an 8-inch tart pan. Chill until the dough is firm. Preheat the oven to 375°. Bake tart until it becomes golden brown and the edges pull away slightly from the sides of the pan, about 20 minutes. Set aside to cool. Freeze until ready to use.

3. To make the mousse, melt the chocolate and butter in a double boiler over simmering water until smooth.

4. Beat the egg yolks in a large bowl and add the chocolate-butter mixture. Stir in the liqueur.

5. Beat the egg whites with cream of tartar to a soft peak and add the sugar gradually. Continue to beat until stiff. Whisk a third of the whites into the chocolate mixture and fold in the rest.

6. Whip the cream and fold it into the mousse. Refrigerate until firm, at least 1 hour.

7. To assemble the tart, spoon the chilled mousse in irregular dollops into the tart shell. Arrange the chocolate curls on top. Chill the tart until ready to serve.

Spinach Soufflé

🌸

MENU
**Spinach Soufflé
Baked Goat Cheese with Salad
Hot Rolls and Sweet Butter
Sautéed Apple Chunks**

With this light soufflé I like to serve a separate first course of cheese and salad (opposite). Little rounds of baked Montrachet cheese served with soft salad greens look delicate on a clear Depression-glass plate.

ℳY FAMILY REALLY ENJOYS A soufflé every now and then. They consider it a treat when a puffy, golden spinach or cheese soufflé is served hot from the oven. Contrary to common belief, a soufflé is really not that difficult to master once some basic rules are learned. It is very important to preheat the oven to the correct temperature, in this case 400°.

Make the filling thick enough but not too heavy, and beat the egg whites until stiff and firm but not dry. Egg whites should always be beaten in a clean bowl with a clean beater. Once beaten, the egg whites must be folded into the soufflé filling mixture with a large rubber spatula, with care taken to deflate the whites as little as possible. I like to bake soufflés in tinned charlotte molds, and because I prefer a showy, high soufflé, I sometimes make a collar of waxed paper to tie around the mold. In that case, I fill the mold almost to the top with the soufflé. If I do not build a collar, I fill the mold three quarters full. Once in the oven (the shelf should be in the lower third), the soufflé should remain undisturbed until ready to be removed. It helps if you have a window in your oven door, but if you don't, check after 25 minutes, not before. The soufflé will be done if it is nicely puffed, golden brown on top, and not shaky or wet-looking in the center. I prefer soufflés to be moist in the center but not wet.

This soufflé is preceded by an unusual first course. Rounds of goat cheese are coated with fine bread crumbs and baked until soft and golden. They are served alongside a tender, leafy salad dressed with a balsamic vinegar dressing.

For dessert, sautéed apple chunks are easy and delicious with ice cream.

Spinach Soufflé

SERVES 4

5 tablespoons unsalted butter
1 tablespoon freshly grated
   Parmesan cheese
1 small yellow onion, minced
3/4 cup chopped steamed spinach, or
   one 10-ounce package, thawed
1 1/2 teaspoons kosher salt
   Pinch of cayenne pepper
3 tablespoons flour
1 cup milk, scalded
   Freshly ground black pepper to
   taste
4 large egg yolks
8 egg whites
1/2 cup grated Swiss cheese

1. Preheat oven to 400°. Butter a 6- or 8-cup soufflé dish with 1 tablespoon softened butter and sprinkle with Parmesan cheese.

2. Sauté onion in 1 tablespoon butter for 2 minutes. Add drained spinach, 1/2 teaspoon salt, and cayenne pepper.

3. In a medium saucepan combine remaining 3 tablespoons butter and the flour and cook 2 minutes. Stir in milk, 1/2 teaspoon salt, and black pepper. Stirring continuously, cook 2 minutes. Remove from heat and beat in egg yolks, one at a time. Cook an additional 2 minutes over low flame. Fold in spinach mixture.

4. Beat egg whites with remaining 1/2 teaspoon salt until stiff; fold a quarter of the egg whites into the spinach mixture. Stir in all but 1 tablespoon of the Swiss cheese. Fold in remaining whites and spoon into prepared mold. Top with remaining cheese.

5. Bake 25 to 30 minutes, or until puffed and golden brown. Serve immediately.

Baked Goat Cheese with Salad

SERVES 4

8 *rounds of goat cheese, cut about 3/4 inch thick from a log of Montrachet*
1/2 *cup olive oil*
4 *sprigs fresh thyme*
3/4 *cup fine white bread crumbs*
1 *teaspoon thyme leaves, fresh or dried*
1/4 *teaspoon salt (optional)*
Freshly ground pepper to taste
3 *tablespoons balsamic vinegar*
Assortment of arugula and Bibb, oak leaf, and ruby lettuce (1 large handful per person)

1. Arrange cheese in a shallow dish. Combine oil and sprigs of thyme, pour over the cheese, and marinate for several hours or overnight.

2. Preheat oven to 350°.

3. Combine bread crumbs, thyme leaves, salt, and pepper. Roll the rounds of goat cheese in this, put them in a baking dish, and bake for 15 minutes, or until the cheese is softened and crumbs are golden.

4. Meanwhile, combine oil from the marinade with the vinegar and salt and pepper to taste. Pour over the greens and toss well.

5. Serve the salad on individual plates with two slices of warm goat cheese on the side.

Sautéed Apple Chunks

SERVES 4

3 *McIntosh or Granny Smith apples*
4 *tablespoons (1/2 stick) unsalted butter*
2 *tablespoons honey*
Ice cream (optional)

1. Core apples and cut into chunks.

2. In a medium skillet melt butter over low heat and sauté the apples for 5 to 8 minutes.

3. Drizzle honey over the apples and serve hot with your favorite ice cream, if you like.

Winter

Broiled Steak with Béarnaise Sauce

We have been consuming less and less red meat in our home over the last two or three years, but every now and then we get a craving for a good steak. I buy what looks good from the butcher—a porterhouse, a small sirloin, or even two shell steaks if I feel like splurging. I like to get a steak with a bone in it so that the dogs, Harry and Zuzu, can share in our treat.

We have a Garland range in the house kitchen, which has an excellent broiler. I preheat it so that the steak cooks very quickly once it is put in the broiler. A light simple béarnaise, pan-sautéed spinach subtly flavored with garlic, and buttery baked potatoes complete this no-fuss dinner. This is another dinner menu that is easy to multiply for unexpected guests or additional children home for a holiday.

The crêpes, served with granulated sugar, butter, and Grand Marnier, are one of our favorite desserts. If you wish, melt a bit of apricot preserves over a low flame and spoon them along with the Grand Marnier and butter over the cooked crêpes. Crêpe batter can be made the evening before, or right after you put the potatoes in the oven to bake. Crêpe batter works best if it has at least an hour to rest in the refrigerator before being used.

It's fun to serve an informal meal on such a formal plate. I love to collect all kinds of salt cellars, antique and modern, glass and stoneware. Here, a cut-glass cellar adds an elegant note. Bordeaux wine would be perfect for this meal.

MENU

Broiled Steak with Béarnaise Sauce
Baked Potato
Pan-Sautéed Spinach and Garlic
Grand Marnier Crêpes

Broiled Steak with Béarnaise Sauce

SERVES 2

2 shell steaks, 3/4 pound each
1 tablespoon (1/8 stick) unsalted
   butter

BÉARNAISE SAUCE
(Makes 1/2 cup)

1/4 cup red wine vinegar
1/4 cup dry white wine
1 1/2 tablespoons shallots, minced
1/2 tablespoon dried tarragon
   Salt and freshly ground pepper
    to taste
3 egg yolks
1 tablespoon lemon juice
1 stick unsalted butter, melted
2 tablespoons minced fresh
   tarragon or parsley

1. Preheat broiler.

2. To make the sauce, boil vinegar, wine, shallots, dried tarragon, and salt and pepper in a small saucepan until reduced to about 2 tablespoons. Strain, reserving the liquid, and cool.

3. In a blender put egg yolks, lemon juice, and reserved liquid. Mix at high speed. Slowly pour in a steady stream of melted butter as the mixer runs. When all is well blended, pour sauce into a bowl. Stir in minced herbs and correct seasonings. Set aside.

4. Put steaks on a broiler rack and broil on each side for 5 minutes. The steak will be rare.

5. Dot the steaks with butter, season to taste, and serve immediately with béarnaise sauce.

Baked Potato

SERVES 2

Preheat oven to 400°. Put 2 large scrubbed baking potatoes in the center of the oven and bake until tender, about 45 to 50 minutes. Serve with bowls of unsalted butter, coarse salt, sour cream, and finely chopped fresh chives.

Pan-Sautéed Spinach and Garlic

SERVES 2

> 2 tablespoons (1/4 stick) unsalted butter
> 1 clove garlic, peeled and minced
> 1 pound fresh spinach, trimmed, washed, and well drained
> Coarse salt and freshly ground pepper to taste

1. Melt butter in a large frying pan over medium heat, add garlic, and cook for 2 minutes.

2. Add spinach and sauté over high heat until wilted. Remove from heat. Season and serve at once.

Grand Marnier Crêpes

MAKES 8 TO 10 CRÊPES

1/4 cup sugar
1/4 cup Grand Marnier
1/4 cup (1/4 stick) unsalted butter, melted

CRÊPE BATTER

> 3/4 cup cold water
> 3/4 cup milk
> 3 eggs
> 1/4 teaspoon salt
> 1 1/2 cups flour
> 3 tablespoons unsalted butter, melted
> 1 teaspoon Grand Marnier

1. In a blender mix all the batter ingredients at high speed for 2 minutes. Pour into a bowl and refrigerate during dinner.

2. When ready for dessert, heat crêpe pan and lightly butter it. Pour about 1/4 cup batter into the pan, quickly tilting it to run batter over the entire surface. Pour any excess back into the bowl; the crêpes should be thin. Trim the edges.

3. Cook crêpe over medium heat for about 50 seconds on one side, or until it loosens from the pan and is light brown in color. Flip it with your fingers or a spatula and cook for another minute. Both sides should be light brown.

4. Remove crêpe from the pan, sprinkle with sugar, Grand Marnier, and a little melted butter, and roll or fold into quarters. Serve hot.

Kielbasa Simmered in Beer and Onions

Old octagonal Quimper plates from Brittany, hand-painted in an unusual flower pattern, make a charming, old-fashioned table. A platter of sausage and onions, a warm root-vegetable salad, and dark rye bread are set out on a cotton rag rug, contributing to the overall country feeling of this dinner.

Kielbasa Simmered in Beer and Onions
Warm Salad of Winter Vegetables
Rye Bread and Sweet Butter
Clementines and Oatmeal Shortbread

*A*MERICANS OFTEN OVERLOOK ethnic sausages when preparing easy meals. The ubiquitous hot dog somehow tastes better at the ball park or on the street than it does cooked at home, but Polish kielbasa simmered in beer and yellow onions is a hearty and filling repast for a cold winter night.

Serve the sausage with a warm salad of winter vegetables, thick slices of fresh rye bread with sweet butter, and a plate of clementines (small tangerinelike fruits) and oatmeal shortbread for dessert.

Kielbasa Simmered in Beer and Onions

SERVES 4 TO 6

4 tablespoons butter
4 to 5 small onions, thinly sliced
1 2-pound kielbasa
2 12-ounce bottles of beer

1. In a large heavy skillet melt the butter and sauté the onions over medium heat until translucent.

2. Add the kielbasa to the pan and brown it 3 to 4 minutes on each side.

3. Pour the beer over the sausage and onions. Bring to a boil. Reduce the heat and simmer, uncovered, for 25 minutes.

4. Remove the kielbasa and onions from the pan and put them on a serving dish in a warm oven. Reduce the beer over high heat to 2 cups. Pour over the kielbasa and serve.

Warm Salad of Winter Vegetables

SERVES 4 TO 6

2 pint boxes of Brussels sprouts
1 bunch carrots (about 5), peeled
7 to 9 small red or white new
   potatoes
2 scallions, finely chopped

DRESSING (Makes 1 1/2 cups)

1 egg
2 tablespoons Dijon mustard
3 tablespoons cider vinegar
1 tablespoon celery seed
1 tablespoon walnut oil (optional)
3/4 cup vegetable oil
   Salt and pepper to taste

1. In separate pots of lightly salted water cook the Brussels sprouts, carrots, and potatoes until tender but not mushy.

2. In a mixing bowl combine egg, mustard, vinegar, and celery seed. Whisking constantly, add the oil in a slow stream until all is incorporated. Season with salt and pepper.

3. Arrange the vegetables in a salad bowl. Pour the dressing over them and sprinkle with the chopped scallions.

Oatmeal Shortbread

SERVES 4 TO 6

3 1/2 cups rolled oats
2/3 cup brown sugar
1/4 cup all-purpose flour
1/2 teaspoon salt
3/4 cup (1 1/2 sticks) unsalted
   butter, at room temperature
1 teaspoon vanilla extract

1. Preheat the oven to 350°. In a large mixing bowl combine all dry ingredients.

2. Add the butter and vanilla and work them into the flour with a wooden spoon or your fingers until the mixture is crumbly.

3. Press the dough into a well-buttered 9-inch-square baking dish. Bake for 15 minutes until golden. Cool thoroughly before cutting into squares.

Shrimp Tortillas

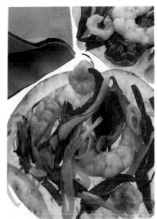

FOR A COLD WINTER EVENING this is an especially inviting menu. My colleague Sara Foster first made the red pepper soup for the publication party of *Entertaining,* and it has become a favorite. Both fresh and roasted peppers are used, and Sara added a pear for sweetness. You can make it as mild or as spicy as you wish.

The shrimp tortillas are an adaptation of a dish I tasted at Craig Claiborne's birthday celebration last fall at his home on Long Island. Many renowned chefs from all over the United States came to prepare his favorite recipes, and the food served ranged from elaborate roasted capons to extremely simple blackened redfish. In Craig's kitchen a fabulous young chef named Zarela Martinez prepared shrimp and langostina tortillas. We serve tortillas often now as a main course and even more often as an hors d'oeuvre. If we can't find very small tortillas, we cut larger ones into fourths for easy handling. I like to use as many different types of peppers as I can— red, yellow, black, and green bell peppers, banana peppers, assorted hot peppers. We are lucky to have lots of peppers in the garden, but many groceries are selling a wide variety of peppers.

Dessert is a refreshing combination of ice and fruit. After the spicy soup and the even spicier tortilla, you will welcome the soothing coolness of tequila ice and ripe papaya.

The spicy peppers in the soup (opposite) and the tortilla (above) make a blustery winter day seem warm and cozy. I like to serve the soup in Andy's pinkware bowls garnished with fresh tarragon. Bright red peppers are so eye-catching that they make a wonderful centerpiece all by themselves.

❧

MENU
Red Pepper Soup
Shrimp Tortillas
French Bread
Papayas with Tequila Ice

Red Pepper Soup

SERVES 4 TO 6

8 red peppers
3 carrots, peeled
3 shallots, peeled
1 clove garlic, peeled
1 pear, peeled and quartered
1 tablespoon olive oil
4 tablespoons (1/2 stick) unsalted
   butter
1 quart chicken stock
1 teaspoon crushed dried red
   pepper
Dash of cayenne pepper
Salt and black pepper to taste
Sprigs of fresh tarragon, to taste

1. Slice thinly 6 of the peppers, the carrots, shallots, garlic, and pear.

2. Heat the oil and butter in a large skillet and sauté the sliced vegetables and pear over medium-low heat until tender, 8 to 10 minutes.

3. Add the stock, dried red pepper, cayenne pepper, salt and black pepper. Bring to a boil and simmer, covered, for 25 to 30 minutes.

4. While the soup is cooking, roast the remaining red peppers directly on the gas flame,* rotating them with tongs until completely charred. Put them in a paper bag for 5 minutes to sweat. Wash off the blackened skin under cold running water and remove seeds. Drain on paper towel.

5. Purée the soup in a food processor or blender, adding one of the roasted red peppers. Pour the puréed soup back into the pan and reheat over low flame.

6. Julienne the remaining red pepper into fine strips and add them to the soup. Garnish with tarragon and serve with French bread.

   * If gas flame is not available, peppers can be roasted under a hot broiler.

Shrimp Tortillas

SERVES 4

> 12 to 16 large shrimp
> 1/2 cup olive oil
> 1 green pepper, julienned
> 1 red bell pepper, julienned
> 1 banana pepper (a long, pale yellow pepper also called Cubanelle), julienned
> 1 chili pepper, julienned
> 2 cloves garlic, crushed
> 10 assorted small hot chili peppers, whole (jalapeno, cayenne, etc.)
> Salt and freshly ground pepper to taste
> 2 tablespoons olive oil
> 8 to 12 corn tortillas, 6 inches in diameter

1. Clean, shell, and devein shrimp, leaving on tails.

2. In a large skillet heat 1/2 cup oil over medium heat and sauté the julienned peppers and garlic for 2 minutes.

3. Add shrimp and hot chilies and cook for about 3 minutes, or until the shrimp turn bright orange. Do not overcook. Season with salt and pepper.

4. In another skillet heat the 2 tablespoons oil over high heat. Fry tortillas on both sides to desired crispness. Drain on paper towel.*

5. Spoon the shrimp and pepper mixture onto lightly fried tortillas. Serve immediately.

* You can slightly blacken the tortillas over a gas flame instead of frying them. Hold the tortillas with tongs over the flame for a few seconds until each side is slightly blackened. The tortillas will remain softer than if deep fried.

❊

Papayas with Tequila Ice

SERVES 4

> 1 tray ice cubes
> 1/2 cup tequila
> Juice of 4 limes
> Juice of 2 lemons
> 3/4 cup sugar
> 2 papayas, sliced

Combine all ingredients except papayas in a blender and blend until smooth. Serve immediately with papaya slices, or freeze until ready to serve.

Rotelle with Bacon and Sautéed Walnuts

OUR CATERING KITCHEN HAS AN informal system for lunch: whoever feels like cooking searches for a little of this and that and creates what is generally a wonderful lunch. Pasta is very often served, primarily because there is always a large variety of dried and frozen pasta on hand and sauces or toppings can be made rapidly.

One day last winter we were cooking for a very large party and also photographing for the *New York Times*. About fifteen people needed lunch, and Lisa offered to prepare it. She made this marvelous rotelle (corkscrew pasta) dish with sautéed walnuts, bacon, red peppers, eggplants, and zucchini. With it she served a spinach and mushroom salad, to which were added nasturtium leaves, fennel slices, and parsley leaves. The whole lunch took less than half an hour to make, and it was very satisfying. I've made it many times for my family since.

Oysters with a pink butter topping would be an appropriate first course for this menu. Pink butter is a flavored butter sauce known in French as *beurre rouge*. I make it with shallots, red wine or red wine vinegar (or a mixture of both), and lots of unsalted butter. The mixture can be served creamy and smooth, with the shallots strained from the wine mixture, or the shallots can be left in for more texture. The most important thing to remember when making pink butter is that the butter should never get too hot, it should not melt; but rather it should soften into the hot wine mixture. (When white wine or champagne is used the sauce is called *beurre blanc*.)

A good dessert for this meal would be a homemade sorbet made with black currants and crème de cassis.

Bright orange Fiestaware sets off the colors of this interesting pasta dish, accompanied by a classic spinach and mushroom salad. A linen dishtowel makes a wonderful oversized napkin.

✣

MENU
Oysters with Pink Butter
Spinach and Mushroom Salad
Rotelle with Bacon and Sautéed Walnuts
Cassis Sorbet

Oysters with Pink Butter

SERVES 4

10 to 12 oysters in the shell
1 tablespoon shallots, minced
1 tablespoon unsalted butter
1 tablespoon red wine vinegar
5 tablespoons red wine
1 stick of cold unsalted butter cut
into 10 pieces
Salt and pepper to taste
1 bunch chives

1. Place oysters on a hot grill or in an oven until they just begin to open. Open completely with a knife and remove the top shell.

2. While oysters are opening sauté the shallots in 1 tablespoon butter for about 30 seconds. Add the vinegar and wine and reduce the liquid to a third. Remove from the fire and whisk cold butter into the remaining liquid one piece at a time until all is incorporated and mixture is creamy.

3. Add salt, pepper, and chives cut into 1/4-inch pieces and spoon over warm oysters.

Spinach and Mushroom Salad

SERVES 4

A handful of spinach leaves,
stems removed, per person
1/2 pound white mushrooms, stems
sliced off at the level of the cap
Small handful of nasturtium
leaves, if available
1/2 cup thinly sliced fennel bulbs
1/4 cup Italian parsley leaves

DRESSING (Makes 1 cup)

Juice of 1/2 lemon
1 tablespoon champagne or white
wine vinegar
3 tablespoons walnut oil
1/2 cup vegetable oil
Salt and pepper to taste

1. In a large salad bowl arrange spinach, mushrooms, nasturtium leaves, fennel, and parsley.

2. In a small mixing bowl combine all ingredients for the dressing and pour it over the greens. Toss well and serve.

Rotelle with Bacon and Sautéed Walnuts

SERVES 4

> 1 pound rotelle
> 1/2 pound sliced lean bacon, cut into 2-inch pieces
> 1/2 cup walnuts, halved
> 4 tablespoons olive oil
> 4 tablespoons (1/2 stick) unsalted butter
> 2 Japanese eggplants, unpeeled and sliced
> 2 red bell peppers, seeded and cut into strips
> 2 small zucchini, sliced
> Salt and pepper to taste
> Parmesan cheese

1. Cook the pasta in a large pot of boiling salted water until *al dente,* about 12 minutes. Drain and rinse quickly under cold water.

2. Cook bacon in a large skillet until brown and crisp. Remove and drain on paper towel, leaving bacon fat in the pan.

3. In the same skillet, sauté the walnuts over high heat until dark brown. Push to one side of the skillet.

4. In a separate skillet, heat the oil and butter over medium-high flame and quickly sauté, separately, the eggplants, red peppers, and zucchini until brown and tender, about 5 minutes each. Add more oil if necessary.

5. Add pasta and vegetables to the skillet with the walnuts. Heat over medium-high flame and toss well. Adjust seasoning and serve immediately with grated Parmesan cheese.

Cassis Sorbet

MAKES 1 1/2 QUARTS

> 1 jar black currants in heavy syrup (2-pound 1-ounce jar)
> 3 tablespoons sugar
> 3 tablespoons crème de cassis

1. Drain the currants and pour the syrup into a saucepan with the sugar. Bring to a boil and reduce over high heat by a third.

2. Purée the currants in a food processor. Pass the fruit purée through a medium sieve, then through a fine sieve. Discard all skins and seeds.

3. Combine the sieved pulp, crème de cassis, and syrup. Chill thoroughly.

4. Put this mixture in an ice cream machine and proceed according to the manufacturer's directions.

Our 1805 farmhouse has a large cooking fireplace (opposite). In it I constructed a spit from iron hooks, a long skewer, and some wire, which is perfect for grilling certain cuts of meat. The vegetables keep warm next to the fire on old brass and iron trivets, which also serve as little "worktables." A square copper tray (left) holds small balls of Montrachet cheese, which have been coated with herbs and spices, and an assortment of other cheeses and fruits.

Grilled Fillet of Beef with Black Peppercorns

❧

MENU
Grilled Fillet of Beef with Black Peppercorns
Foil-Baked New Potatoes
Chicory Sautéed in Olive Oil and Garlic
Grilled Radicchio
Exceptional Cheese

*F*OR THIS MENU I COATED A

whole fillet of beef in crushed black peppercorns (Malabar or Tellicherry peppercorns are both pungent and aromatic) and olive oil, and then roasted it on a spit in front of a very hot fire. By the time the meat was done, and the potatoes cooked, the fire had died down sufficiently so that I could grill small heads of radicchio, first dipped in sage butter, over the coals. In an old-fashioned cast-iron tripod pan I sautéed chicory in olive oil with a bit of garlic and salt and pepper to serve as an additional vegetable.

❧

Grilled Fillet of Beef with Black Peppercorns

SERVES 6 TO 8

1   2 1/2- to 3-pound fillet of beef
1/4   cup olive oil
4   tablespoons coarsely ground black pepper

1.   Trim all the fat from the fillet.

2.   Rub the meat with olive oil and press the pepper into it.

3.   Insert a spit through the length of the fillet, put it in front of a very hot fire, and cook by radiant heat until the meat is grilled to your taste. This will take anywhere from 15 to 30 minutes, depending on size of the fillet and intensity of the fire.

4.   Transfer meat to a serving board or platter, remove the spit, and carve into serving slices.

Note: For oven roasting, preheat the oven to 450°, put the fillet in a roasting pan, and cook for 18 to 20 minutes for a rare fillet, or longer according to your preference.

❧

Foil-Baked New Potatoes

For each serving, wrap 2 or 3 small new potatoes, 1 tablespoon unsalted butter, a sprig of fresh thyme, and salt and pepper to taste in foil. Put each packet in hot coals (or a preheated 450° oven) and cook until done, 30 to 40 minutes.

Chicory Sautéed in Olive Oil and Garlic

SERVES 6 TO 8

> 1 large head curly chicory
> 1/4 cup olive oil
> 4 cloves garlic, peeled and crushed
> 1 teaspoon coarse salt
> Freshly ground black pepper
> Lemon wedges

1. Wash and thoroughly dry the chicory.

2. In a large skillet heat the oil until hot but not smoking. Add the garlic and cook for 1 to 2 minutes. Do not let it burn.

3. Add the chicory and sauté until wilted and tender. Season with salt and pepper. Serve hot with lemon wedges.

Grilled Radicchio

SERVES 6 TO 8

> Allow 2 to 3 small heads
>   radicchio per person, or 1 large
>   head *
> 1/2 pound (2 sticks) unsalted butter,
>   melted
> 2 to 3 sprigs fresh sage, or 1
>   tablespoon dried
> Freshly ground black pepper

1. Leave small heads of radicchio whole; quarter large heads.

2. Melt the butter in a saucepan and add the sage and pepper.

3. Dip the radicchio into the melted butter, then grill it over hot coals until tender and slightly blackened.

  * Belgian endive can be substituted for the radicchio.

Exceptional Cheese

Cut 1 or 2 Montrachet logs into 1/2-inch slices, and mold each piece into a ball the size of a walnut. Roll each ball in a teaspoon of a single herb or spice (I like to use ground cumin, chopped fresh thyme, fresh or dried dill, paprika, chopped chives, and celery seeds), coating evenly and lightly. Insert a piece of straw into each ball for serving.

   To serve, cover a cheese tray with grape leaves and arrange the cheese balls and a selection of other cheeses, such as Explorateur, Camembert, Pipocrème, and Chèvre, over them. Surround with grapes and pears.

This light but satisfying repast brightens the winter day (opposite) *and is a welcome change from more traditional cold-weather soups and stews.* A dry, full-bodied Meursault wine would complement the menu very well. Comice pears are poached in white wine (left) *and served with small pale amethyst glasses of black currant liqueur.*

Fillet of Sole Wrapped in Spinach

❦

MENU
Fillet of Sole Wrapped in Spinach
Warm Potatoes on Lettuce
Wine-Poached Pears with Black Currant Sauce

*F*OR SOME REASON, THE SPINACH
that is available around February every year is big, leafy, dark green, and tender, perfect for wrapping around gently steamed fillets of sole. I had this dish, or its approximation, in California last year and was impressed with its simplicity, delicacy, and beautiful presentation.

The potatoes for the salad are cooked in the same steamer used for the sole fillets. If you like you can add a purée of spinach to the main course, using the smaller leaves of spinach and the trimmings from the larger leaves. I sometimes add crumbled bacon to puréed spinach for a crunchy texture.

The dessert is poached pears. I prefer using Comice or Packham pears for this dessert because they are large, flavorful, and fine-textured. Bosc pears and Bartletts are fine too, but the fruits must be ripe yet firm, and totally free from bruises; poaching accentuates any defects the fruit may have. Pears can be poached in white wine or champagne for a pale, almost transparent appearance, or in red wine for a more robust, colorful result.

❦

Fillet of Sole Wrapped in Spinach

SERVES 4

4 fillets of sole
2 tablespoons (1/4 stick) unsalted
  butter, at room temperature
Salt and pepper to taste
1/2 pound large spinach leaves,
  washed
4 lemon wedges

1. Dot each fillet with butter. Sprinkle with salt and pepper and fold in half crosswise.

2. Put fillets in a steamer and cook for 5 to 7 minutes. Remove and cool slightly.

3. When fillets are cool enough to handle, wrap each in a spinach leaf. Secure leaf with a toothpick if necessary. Return fillets to the steamer and cook until spinach leaves are wilted but still bright green, about 2 minutes. Serve at once with lemon wedges.

❦

Warm Potatoes on Lettuce

SERVES 4

4 medium-size red new potatoes,
  unpeeled
4 to 6 tender lettuce leaves (ruby
  or Boston)
1 red or yellow pepper, finely
  diced

VINAIGRETTE (Makes 1 cup)

1/2 cup almond or safflower oil
1/4 cup tarragon vinegar
1 tablespoon minced red pepper
1 tablespoon minced yellow
  pepper
Salt and pepper to taste

1. Steam the potatoes until tender, about 10 minutes. Slice each potato into 5 or 6 pieces, keeping each potato separate.

2. Combine all the ingredients for the vinaigrette in a mixing bowl.

3. Arrange lettuce on individual serving plates and put the potatoes and the diced pepper on top. Spoon the vinaigrette over the salad and serve.

Wine-Poached Pears
with Black Currant Sauce

SERVES 4

**4 Comice, Packham, Bartlett, or
Bosc pears, ripe yet firm
1 bottle dry white wine
1 cup sugar
1 cinnamon stick
1 vanilla bean
Zest of 1 lemon**

**BLACK CURRANT SAUCE
(Makes 2 cups)**

**2 cups black currant juice *
1/2 to 3/4 cup sugar
2 tablespoons black currant
liqueur**

1. Carefully peel the pears, leaving the stems intact.

2. In a deep saucepan combine the wine, sugar, cinnamon stick, vanilla bean, and lemon zest and bring to a boil. Reduce heat to simmer and add the pears. The poaching liquid should completely cover the pears while cooking; add water or more wine to cover if necessary.

3. Poach pears until tender, 25 to 35 minutes, and leave them in the liquid until ready to serve.

4. To make the sauce, combine all ingredients and stir over low heat until sugar dissolves. Serve warm or cold, spooned around the pears.

Note: The poaching liquid will keep for several weeks in the refrigerator and can be used again and again. The black currant sauce will also keep for a week in the refrigerator, or can be frozen in 1-cup quantities for future use.

* Use bottled black currant juice, or cook 1 quart fresh black currants with 2 cups water until very soft, then strain.

Fettuccine with Smoked Salmon and Fresh Peas

The lightness and tartness of marinated fillet of sole and grapefruit sections (above) is an unexpected first course in winter and a pleasing contrast to the richness of the cream-sauced pasta (left).

MENU
Sole and Grapefruit à la Sara Foster
Fettuccine with Smoked Salmon and Fresh Peas
Green Salad
Pomegranate Seeds in Grand Marnier

*D*URING THE EARLY MONTHS OF the year citrus fruits are most plentiful and delicious. Pale pink Florida grapefruit, in combination with transparent slices of fillet of sole that have been marinated in a gentle mixture of champagne or white wine vinegar, oils, and lime, makes an unusual and refreshing first course. To section the grapefruit for this or any other recipe, peel the whole fruit, removing as much of the white outer membrane as possible. With a very sharp knife cut out each section of fruit, slicing as close to the inner membranes as you can. This is the quickest method of sectioning citrus fruits, but it is not as thorough or as painstaking as other methods.

Spinach fettuccine tossed with smoked salmon and peas in a creamy salmon-flavored sauce is quite easy to prepare. If you can't find fresh peas, substitute frozen petits pois. Use high-quality smoked salmon that is not overly salty.

Because pomegranates are very messy to eat, they seem like a great luxury when peeled and separated into individual seeds and served in cut-glass goblets, doused with Grand Marnier.

❧

Sole and Grapefruit à la Sara Foster

SERVES 4

1 lime
1 fillet of sole (about 1/2 pound)
1 tablespoon champagne or white wine vinegar
1 clove garlic, minced
1/4 cup walnut oil
1/2 cup vegetable oil
Fresh chives
Salt and pepper to taste
1 pink grapefruit

1. Remove the zest from the lime and reserve. Squeeze out the juice, strain, and reserve.

2. Thinly slice the fillet of sole at an angle as you would smoked salmon. Put slices in a shallow dish.

3. Combine lime juice and zest, vinegar, garlic, oils, chives, and salt and pepper. Pour this over the fish and refrigerate for 2 to 3 hours, or preferably overnight.

4. Before serving, peel and section the grapefruit, removing the membrane. Arrange the grapefruit segments and fish on individual plates and pour the remaining vinaigrette over them.

❧

Fettuccine with Smoked Salmon and Fresh Peas

SERVES 4

1 1/2 pounds fresh or dried spinach
fettuccine
2 tablespoons olive oil
1 cup fresh peas
1/4 pound smoked salmon, thinly
sliced
1 pint heavy cream
1 tablespoon minced shallots
2 tablespoons Dubonnet or white
wine
Salt and pepper to taste

1. Cook pasta in a large kettle of lightly salted boiling water until it is *al dente,* or to taste. Drain and toss lightly with olive oil. Set aside in a warm place.

2. Blanch the peas in a pot of lightly salted boiling water for 3 minutes. Drain and plunge into ice water. Drain again. Set aside.

3. Put 4 slices smoked salmon, 2 tablespoons cream, and the shallots in a blender and purée until smooth and creamy. Set aside.

4. Bring the Dubonnet to a boil in heavy saucepan. Add the remaining cream and cook, stirring constantly, until the mixture coats the back of a spoon. Add the salmon purée and blend thoroughly. Stir over low heat until mixture is hot. Season with salt and pepper.

5. Cut the remaining salmon into thin strips. In a large serving dish toss the pasta with the peas and the salmon. Pour the hot sauce over it, toss well, and serve immediately.

❧

Pomegranate Seeds in Grand Marnier

SERVES 4

Peel 2 large, very red pomegranates and, without breaking them, carefully separate the seeds from the white membrane. Fill 4 small goblets (saucer-shaped champagne glasses are nice) with the seeds and pour 3 tablespoons Grand Marnier over each. Set aside until ready to serve.

Oven-Braised Ham Steak

My FAMILY LOVES HAM, AND yet I rarely have the time to serve a whole baked ham. Whenever I purchase one of my favorite smoked Polish Kurowycky hams, I cut off a few steaks to keep in the freezer for a quick and easy winter dinner.

My mother taught me how to make potato pancakes—we used to make mounds of them for our large family and serve them with bowls of sour cream, sautéed onions, and freshly cooked applesauce—and the recipe here is virtually the same one we used in Nutley, New Jersey, where I grew up. For the applesauce use tart, crisp apples for the best results, and little or no sugar.

You can also add a steamed green vegetable such as Brussels sprouts to the menu, tossed with butter, salt, and pepper. A hint: both sprouts and pearl onions cook more quickly when an X is cut in the bottom of each one.

If your family likes chocolate, serve some chocolate brownies for dessert, topped with a bit of whipped cream. The brownies can be made while you're preparing the rest of the meal, or removed from the store of frozen desserts in your freezer.

The rough texture of an unusual hand-crafted earthenware dish with a sandy rim makes this old-fashioned meal even homier.

MENU
Oven-Braised Ham Steak
Quick Applesauce
Potato Pancakes
Steamed Brussels Sprouts
Chocolate Chocolate-Chip Brownies

Oven-Braised Ham Steak

SERVES 4

2 tablespoons (1/4 stick) unsalted
 butter
2 tablespoons brown sugar
4 tablespoons Dijon mustard
3/4 cup dry sherry
1 2-pound ham steak

1. Preheat oven to 325°. Melt butter over low heat in a covered casserole or ovenproof skillet. Add sugar, mustard, and sherry. Stir until the sauce is smooth.

2. Put the ham steak in the pan and spoon the sauce over it. Cover and bake for 30 to 40 minutes. Uncover, baste, and continue to bake until the ham is glazed, 5 to 10 minutes more. Do not overcook. Serve immediately.

Quick Applesauce

SERVES 4

12 tart apples, cored, peeled, and
 chopped
1/2 cup water
 Grated rind of 1 lemon
1 teaspoon honey (optional)
1 teaspoon cinnamon

1. Put the apples and water in a saucepan, cover, and cook over medium heat until apples are soft, 15 to 20 minutes.

2. Mash apples with a heavy spoon. Stir in the lemon rind, honey, and cinnamon. Serve warm.

Potato Pancakes

SERVES 4

4 large baking potatoes
1 medium-size yellow onion
2 eggs, slightly beaten
1/2 cup beer
3 tablespoons flour
2 teaspoons kosher salt
 Freshly ground pepper to taste
 Vegetable oil for frying
 Sour cream

1. Peel and coarsely grate the potatoes. Drain well in a colander over a bowl for a few minutes. Reserve the liquid.

2. Transfer potatoes to another bowl. Skim milky, foamy residue from drained liquid and add it back to the potatoes.

3. Grate the onion into the bowl with the potatoes. Stir in eggs, beer, flour, salt, and pepper.

4. In a heavy skillet heat 1/4 inch oil. When the oil is hot, spoon 1/2 cup of potato mixture per pancake into the skillet. Make a few at a time, being careful they don't run into each other.

5. Fry on both sides until golden brown (about 4 to 6 minutes total) and drain on paper towel. Keep them warm while preparing the others. Serve hot with dollops of sour cream.

Chocolate Chocolate-Chip Brownies

MAKES SIXTEEN 2-INCH-SQUARE BROWNIES

1/2 cup (1 stick) unsalted butter
2 1-ounce squares unsweetened chocolate
1 cup sugar
1/2 cup flour, sifted
1/2 cup chopped pecans or walnuts
1/2 teaspoon baking powder
1 teaspoon vanilla extract
2 eggs, slightly beaten
1 cup semisweet chocolate chips

1. Preheat oven to 350°. Butter an 8-inch-square glass pan.

2. Melt the butter and unsweetened chocolate in the top of a double boiler. Remove from the heat and stir well. (Or you can melt the butter and chocolate in the oven.)

3. In a mixing bowl combine the butter-chocolate with the sugar, flour, nuts, baking powder, and vanilla. Stir well with a wooden spoon.

4. Add the eggs and mix thoroughly. Stir in the chocolate chips.

5. Pour the batter into the prepared pan and bake for 30 to 40 minutes, or until a toothpick inserted in the center comes out clean. Do not overcook. The brownies should be moist and chewy. Cool thoroughly before cutting into 2-inch squares.

Note: These brownies freeze extremely well. Wrap them in plastic wrap. Thaw them in their wrappings.

Mahagony Fried Chicken

*E*VERYONE LOVES FRIED CHICK-
en, and homemade is best. Somewhere long ago I read a recipe for a dish
called mahogany fried chicken, and the following is my remembrance of it.
Correctly, the chicken should be soaked in rich milk or buttermilk for 6
hours or overnight. However, if the chicken is very fresh, a quick soaking—
10 minutes—in milk is sufficient. The chickens should be broilers or small
fryers cut into eighths, the backbones removed. Lots of freshly ground black
pepper will enliven the flour coating, and the frying oil should be a light,
very good quality vegetable oil (I prefer safflower oil). The largest pieces
take no more than 16 minutes to cook and when done are a rich, dark
mahogany brown.

The herb-flavored root vegetables are delicious. Cooked separately in a
Chinese layered steamer and then tossed together with butter and herbs,
they are colorful and healthful. (The same vegetables can be tossed in a hot
vinaigrette with celery seeds and herbs and presented as a "root salad.")

For dessert, individual custards baked in old-fashioned custard cups
seem just right. The addition of dried apricots, golden raisins, and fragrant
nutmeg makes this recipe unusual.

*The warm colors of this
hearty winter menu
(opposite) are accen-
tuated by bright yellow
Fiestaware. Above: rich,
creamy custard, flavored
with dried apricots, golden
raisins, and nutmeg, hot
from the oven.*

MENU
Mahogany Fried Chicken
Herb-Flavored Root Vegetables
Tossed Salad
Quick Cranberry-Orange Relish
Custard with Apricots and Golden Raisins

✥

Mahogany Fried Chicken

SERVES 6

2 2 1/2 pound broiler (or fryer) chickens, each cut into 8 pieces, backbones removed
1 quart buttermilk (whole milk may be substituted)
2 cups all-purpose flour
1 teaspoon salt
1 tablespoon freshly ground black pepper
4 to 6 cups safflower oil or any good-quality vegetable oil

1. Soak the chicken pieces in buttermilk overnight (or at least 6 hours) before cooking.

2. To prepare the chicken, combine the flour with salt and pepper. Dredge chicken pieces in flour and shake off excess.

3. In a skillet heat 2 inches of oil to 350°. Fry the chicken pieces, a few at a time, for 12 to 16 minutes, turning them every 3 to 4 minutes. When the skin becomes deep mahogany in color, remove the pieces from the skillet and drain on a rack or paper towels. Serve hot, warm, or cold.

✥

Quick Cranberry-Orange Relish

MAKES 2 CUPS

In the bowl of a food processor combine 1 pound fresh cranberries, the rind and pulp of one orange, ½ cup walnuts, and sugar to taste. Process just until coarsely chopped. Let the relish sit at least 30 minutes before serving. Left-over relish can be refrigerated for a few days and is also delicious with roast turkey, pork, or ham.

Herb-Flavored Root Vegetables

SERVES 6

       1   cup sweet potatoes, cut into
           1-inch cubes
       1   cup white potatoes, cut into
           1-inch cubes
       1   cup parsnips, cut into 1-inch
           cubes
       1   cup carrots, cut into 1-inch cubes
       1   cup turnips, cut into 1-inch
           cubes
       4   tablespoons (1/2 stick) unsalted
           butter
           Salt and pepper to taste
     1/2   teaspoon fresh or dried chives,
           thyme or dill

1. Steam vegetables separately in a layered Chinese steamer.

2. Toss the vegetables with butter, salt and pepper, and thyme. Serve hot.

Custard with Apricots and Golden Raisins

SERVES 6

       1   cup sugar
       3   eggs
       3   egg yolks
   1 1/4   cups heavy cream
   1 1/4   cups milk
       1   vanilla bean, split
     1/2   cup dried apricots
     1/2   cup golden raisins
     1/4   teaspoon nutmeg

1. Preheat the oven to 325°. In a mixing bowl combine the sugar, eggs, and egg yolks. Beat with a whisk until creamy and pale yellow.

2. In a small saucepan combine the cream and milk. Add the vanilla bean and bring to a boil. Remove the bean and pour the liquid into the eggs.

3. Butter a 1 1/2-quart shallow baking dish (or 6 individual custard molds) and pour in the egg mixture. Sprinkle the apricots and raisins over it. Dust with nutmeg.

4. Put the baking dish in a deep baking or roasting pan. Fill the pan with boiling water so it reaches about halfway up the sides of the custard dish. Bake until the custard is set, 45 minutes to 1 hour. Cool before serving.

Veal Piccata

WHEN I WAS A STOCKBROKER ON
Wall Street I was actually required to take clients out to fancy lunches and
dinners as part of the job. It was in the dining rooms of New York's most
famous restaurants that I was introduced to *haute cuisine,* and in the kitchens
of those restaurants that I learned much about cooking. I would frequently
eat something delicious at lunch, ask about the recipe or unusual ingredients, and rush home after work to re-create the recipe for my family.

At Orsini's I often enjoyed the veal piccata, thin tender slices of the
whitest veal lightly cooked in butter and oil and flavored with lemon and
pepper. I make veal piccata at home whenever I happen to see especially
high-quality veal.

With the veal I like to serve orzo, a small egg-shaped pasta, and grated
zucchini tossed with hot garlic butter and nutmeg. If you wish, you can add
a salad of fresh spinach with toasted almonds, bacon, and an almond oil
vinaigrette.

For dessert serve a very rich, puddinglike soufflé of chocolate, hot from
the oven. Once you master the basics of soufflés, you will find they are easy
to create in a variety of flavors, sweet or savory.

*There is nothing so fresh
and appealing as red-
and-white gingham for the
table. I use it here with
white ironstone plates and
one of my milk-glass
nesting hens.*

MENU
Veal Piccata
Orzo with Sautéed Onions
Grated Zucchini
Spinach, Almond, and Bacon Salad
Chocolate Soufflé

Veal Piccata

SERVES 4

1/4 cup flour
1 pound leg of veal, sliced very thin (less than 1/4 inch thick) into 3-by-4-inch pieces
1/4 cup vegetable oil
2 tablespoons (1/4 stick) unsalted butter
Juice of 1 lemon
1/4 cup dry white wine
1 lemon
Salt and pepper to taste

1. Lightly flour veal on both sides. Shake off excess.

2. In a large heavy skillet heat oil and butter. When bubbling, add veal and sauté about 2 minutes on each side. When the veal is nearly cooked, sprinkle on lemon juice. Remove veal from the pan and keep warm.

3. Add wine to the pan and deglaze over high heat, stirring constantly. Reduce liquid to about 3 tablespoons. Pour sauce over veal.

4. Slice the lemon to paper thinness and put a slice on each veal scallop. Sprinkle with salt and pepper. Serve at once.

Orzo with Sautéed Onions

SERVES 4

2 quarts water
1 teaspoon salt
1 cup orzo (tiny Greek pasta beads, available in gourmet stores)
3 tablespoons unsalted butter
2 medium onions, chopped

1. In a large pot bring salted water to a boil. Add orzo and cook for 12 minutes, or until just tender. Drain.

2. In a skillet melt butter and sauté onions over medium heat for about 4 minutes.

3. Add the orzo to the onions. Stir well and serve immediately.

Grated Zucchini

SERVES 4

2 tablespoons (1/4 stick) unsalted
butter
1 small clove garlic, peeled and
diced
3 medium zucchini, unpeeled,
grated
Freshly grated nutmeg
Salt and pepper to taste

1. In a large skillet melt the butter and sauté the garlic over medium heat for 3 to 4 minutes. Do not brown.

2. Toss the zucchini in the hot garlic butter until tender, 2 to 3 minutes. Season with nutmeg and salt and pepper, and serve immediately.

Chocolate Soufflé

SERVES 4

1 tablespoon instant espresso
1 tablespoon hot water
6 ounces semisweet chocolate
1/4 cup heavy cream
3 egg yolks
1 tablespoon flour
6 egg whites
Pinch of cream of tartar
2 tablespoons sugar

1. Preheat oven to 325°. Butter and flour 2 1/2-pint soufflé mold. Chill until ready to use.

2. Combine espresso with hot water and stir until it is dissolved. Set aside.

3. Melt the chocolate on top of a double boiler over simmering water. Stir in the cream and coffee.

4. In a small bowl beat the egg yolks and flour. Stir this into the chocolate.

5. In another bowl beat the egg whites with cream of tartar to a soft peak. Sprinkle in the sugar, a little at a time, and beat to a stiff peak.

6. Stir a quarter of the whites into the chocolate mixture, then fold the chocolate mixture into the remaining egg whites, a little at a time. Pour this into the prepared soufflé mold.

7. Bake for 35 to 45 minutes, or until a knife inserted into the edge of the soufflé comes out clean. Serve hot with lightly whipped cream.

Fried Oyster Sandwiches

SOFT GREENS AND PALE PUR-
ples are colors associated with Laura Ashley, the designer of women's fash-
ions and fabrics. When my staff and I made this soup we immediately
named it "Laura Ashley soup" because of its extraordinary color. The
cooked red cabbage, when puréed with the other ingredients, turned a
lovely shade of lavender. This soup is delicious, delicate yet hearty. The
julienned leeks and red cabbage add texture and color, and the parsnips add
that depth of flavor necessary to good soup.

The fried oyster sandwiches are a very special treat. Use plump, fresh
oysters and fry them very lightly with a coating of cornmeal and flour. The
combination of fresh oysters with mashed and unmashed avocados and
fresh coriander (cilantro) on toasted French bread is terrific.

The carrot salad is made a bit more interesting by the addition of
mandarin orange sections. In winter you can often buy mandarin oranges;
out of season, used the canned sections, well drained of the sweet syrup.
For dessert, serve huge Cortland apples, baked until tender with brown
sugar and spices. I like to use the largest apples I can find, and I always
make extras because they are so good for snacks or breakfast the next day.

*The delicate hues of this
"Laura Ashley soup" look
best on a perfectly plain
old Staffordshire cream-
ware soup plate. A
Japanese silk obi in
dark, muted shades picks
up the colors in the soup
and makes a wonderful
table covering.*

MENU
Cabbage-Leek Soup
Fried Oyster Sandwiches
Carrot and Mandarin Orange Salad
Baked Cortland Apples with Maple Yogurt

Cabbage-Leek Soup

SERVES 4 TO 6

8 small leeks
6 tablespoons (3/4 stick) unsalted
   butter
2 cups chopped red cabbage
6 cloves garlic, chopped
2 parsnips, peeled and chopped
4 cups chicken stock
1 cup shredded red cabbage
   Salt and pepper to taste

1. Julienne 3 of the leeks, including the green part. Set aside. Coarsely chop the whites of the remaining leeks.

2. Melt 4 tablespoons butter over medium-low heat in a large pot. Cook the chopped leeks, red cabbage, garlic, and parsnips until tender, about 15 minutes. Add chicken stock to the vegetables, bring to a boil, reduce to simmer, and cook for 35 minutes. Purée the soup in a food processor.

3. Sauté the shredded cabbage and julienned leeks in the remaining butter for 3 minutes, or until their colors become bright. Reheat the soup, season, and stir in the leeks and cabbage. Serve immediately.

Fried Oyster Sandwiches

PER SANDWICH

2 or 3 oysters, shucked
2 tablespoons flour for dredging
1 egg, lightly beaten
2 tablespoons cornmeal
   Peanut oil for frying
1/2 ripe avocado
   Juice of 1/2 lemon or lime
   Hot chili oil to taste
2 to 3 sprigs fresh coriander
   Salt and pepper to taste
   French bread

1. Dredge the oysters in the flour. Shake off the excess. Dip them in the egg, then in the cornmeal.

2. In a saucepan heat the oil until very hot but not smoking. Fry the oysters until golden brown, 3 to 4 minutes. Drain on paper towels.

3. In a mixing bowl mash 1/2 of the avocado half and combine with lemon juice, hot chili oil, half the coriander (chopped), and salt and pepper.

4. Slice the bread and heat slightly. Spread the avocado mixture on 1 slice. On the other, arrange the oysters and the rest of the avocado, thinly sliced. Make a sandwich and garnish with the rest of the coriander leaves.

Carrot and Mandarin Orange Salad

SERVES 4 TO 6

4 to 5 carrots
5 to 6 sprigs fresh tarragon
2 mandarin oranges

VINAIGRETTE (Makes 3/4 cup)

2 tablespoons Grand Marnier
1 tablespoon white wine vinegar
1/4 cup olive oil
1/4 cup vegetable oil
2 tablespoons honey
1 tablespoon mustard

1. Peel the carrots and julienne into very fine strips, or grate them in a food processor. Put the carrots in a salad bowl. Remove the leaves from the tarragon sprigs and julienne them into fine strips. Add to carrots.

2. Peel and section the oranges. Remove all the membranes, leaving only the pulp, and add to the carrots and tarragon.

3. In a small mixing bowl combine all the ingredients for the vinaigrette. Stir well, pour over the salad, and toss.

Baked Cortland Apples with Maple Yogurt

1 APPLE PER PERSON

1 apple
2 tablespoons brown sugar
1 tablespoon butter
1/2 teaspoon cinnamon
Pinch of freshly grated nutmeg
Pinch of ground mace
Yogurt or whipped cream
Maple syrup

1. Preheat the oven to 375°. Cut off the top of the apple and core it, taking care not to cut through the bottom skin. Fill the cavity with the sugar, butter, cinnamon, nutmeg, and mace. Put the apple in a shallow baking dish with 1/2 inch boiling water on the bottom. Bake until the apple is tender but not mushy, about 35 to 40 minutes.

2. Serve with yogurt or lightly whipped cream that has been sweetened with maple syrup.

Beef Liver with Sage

The focal point of this table setting for two is an exotic handwoven nineteenth-century Kashmir shawl, which I have used for a table covering. Creamy white Fiestaware plates hold the meal of baby beef liver, butter-and-cream-tossed fettuccine, braised scallions and Jerusalem artichokes, and yellow pear tomato salad. Cobalt blue American glasses and a sprig of sage blossoms add the only touch of color needed.

❧

MENU

Beef Liver with Sage
Fettuccine Tossed with Butter and Cream
Braised Scallions and Jerusalem Artichokes
Baby Lettuce with Yellow Pear Tomatoes
Vanilla Ice Cream and Boysenberry Sherbet Parfaits

*W*HEN ANDY AND I WERE IN northern Italy, somewhere near Lake Como, we were served beef liver that had been sautéed with sage (*salvia* in Italian). We had grown sage for years in our herb garden, but neither of us had ever tasted sautéed sage. Since then I have used sage often in the preparation of meats and fish. I like to cook branches of sage in hot olive oil—they become crispy and are very good to eat with roasted chicken or veal. I chop up sage leaves to use in stuffings and fillings. And sage leaves, which come in purple, green, gray, and variegated shades, are an excellent, long-lasting garnish.

To accompany the sautéed liver I like to serve braised scallions with rounds of Jerusalem artichoke, and fettuccine.

For a salad, try a mixture of baby lettuce with halves of yellow pear tomatoes instead of the ubiquitous red cherry tomato. For dessert, make parfaits of boysenberry sherbet and vanilla ice cream.

❧

Beef Liver with Sage

SERVES 2

> 3/4 pound baby beef liver, sliced less than 1/4 inch thick (if you wish, you can use calves' liver)
> 1/2 cup milk
> 1/2 cup all-purpose flour
> Salt and pepper to taste
> 4 tablespoons (1/2 stick) unsalted butter
> 2 tablespoons olive oil
> 10 to 12 fresh or dried sage leaves

1. Cut the sliced liver into strips about 1 inch wide. Soak them in the milk for about 20 minutes.

2. Combine the flour with salt and pepper. Lightly dredge the liver strips in it.

3. In a large skillet heat the butter and oil until hot but not smoking. Quickly sauté the liver until golden brown, about 5 minutes.

4. Remove the liver strips with a slotted spoon and put on a serving platter. Keep them warm. In the same skillet sauté the sage leaves briefly, about 1 minute. Spoon them over the liver and serve.

Fettuccine Tossed with Butter and Cream

SERVES 2

1/2 pound fresh or dried fettuccine
4 tablespoons (1/2 stick) unsalted butter
3/4 cup heavy cream
2 egg yolks
Salt and pepper to taste
Freshly grated Parmesan cheese to taste
Sprig of fresh rosemary (optional)

1. Cook the fettuccine in a large pot of boiling salted water until *al dente* (firm, yet tender). Drain.

2. In a large skillet melt the butter, add the cream and sprig of rosemary, and bring to a boil.

3. In a large bowl beat the egg yolks and pour in the cream mixture, a little at a time, whisking constantly. Remove the rosemary. Add the fettuccine and toss well, coating it completely. Return everything to the skillet and cook over medium heat, stirring constantly, to warm the pasta. Season with salt and pepper and Parmesan cheese. Serve hot.

Braised Scallions and Jerusalem Artichokes

SERVES 2 TO 3

8 to 10 Jerusalem artichokes
1 bunch scallions
1/4 cup water
3/4 stick unsalted butter
1/2 cup Dubonnet Blanc or dry vermouth
Salt and pepper to taste

1. Put the Jerusalem artichokes in the top of a steamer and cook them for 5 minutes. Cool.

2. Clean and trim the scallions, leaving on the roots. When the artichokes are cool enough to handle, peel them into smooth rounds about the size of a chestnut.

3. Put the water and half of the butter in a sauté pan. Bring to a boil, add the scallions and Jerusalem artichokes, and cook over high heat for about 5 minutes. The water should evaporate to 1 tablespoon. If not, discard the excess liquid.

4. Add remaining butter to the pan and lightly brown the vegetables. Remove the vegetables to a heated platter. Deglaze the pan with Dubonnet and pour over the vegetables. Season with salt and pepper and serve hot.

I love the soft glow of candlelight in the evening and like to group a variety of candles and cut-glass holders in the entrance foyer of our home. The showy roasted chicken (opposite) looks particularly dramatic in this setting. A turn-of-the-century Japanese dessert set (left) displays an unpeeled sugar-glazed pear in cream. An antique salt cellar holds brown English rock sugar for the tea.

Herb-Roasted Chicken with Baked Shallots

❧

MENU
Herb-Roasted Chicken with Baked Shallots
Mashed Sweet Potatoes
Pears Baked in Cream

*A*T ONE TIME, MOST OF US would probably not have dreamed of roasting an entire chicken as a Quick Cook meal. Somehow, roast chicken was always reminiscent of leisurely Sunday dinners, when the bird was put into the oven, heavily stuffed with bread and onion and celery, and slowly roasted for hours to ultimate succulence. Nowadays, though, we have learned that chicken can be just as delicious stuffed with simple herbs and roasted undisturbed, except for one or two bastings, for only an hour, making it an ideal quick meal.

To further simplify the meal, cook the vegetables right in the pan with chicken. For this meal I peeled lots of whole shallots and garlic. You could add other vegetables such as carrots, whole or cut onions, potatoes, turnips, or Brussels sprouts. A bit of white wine added during the roasting aids in the basting and heightens the flavor of the chicken. I like to roast one 5- or 6-pound bird or two or three smaller chickens.

Sweet potatoes are baked in the oven with the chicken after being boiled for 20 minutes. The boiling brings out the sweetness of the potatoes and the roasting caramelizes the natural sugars. The flesh is scraped from the skins and mashed coarsely. I season the potato with butter, thyme, and nutmeg. If you prefer, serve the chicken with two or three vegetable purées —carrot and rutabaga, turnip and pear, parsnip and potato: very good combinations and easy to prepare.

Dessert is half a pear, unpeeled and baked in the oven with a bit of cream, sugar, and butter. Use brown-skinned Bosc pears or golden or red Bartletts.

Mashed Sweet Potatoes

SERVES 4

6 medium-size sweet potatoes
4 tablespoons (1/2 stick) unsalted butter
4 sprigs fresh thyme
Salt and pepper to taste
Freshly grated nutmeg to taste

1. Cook the sweet potatoes for 20 minutes in lightly salted water. Drain.

2. Put the potatoes in the oven with the chicken and roast them until they are very tender.

3. Halve the potatoes, scoop out the flesh, and mash with a fork.

4. Melt the butter with the thyme in a small saucepan. Remove the thyme sprigs and reserve. Stir the melted butter into the mashed potatoes and season with salt and pepper and nutmeg. Garnish with the thyme sprigs.

Herb-Roasted Chicken with Baked Shallots

SERVES 4

> 1 5- to 6-pound roasting chicken
>   Kosher salt and freshly ground
>   pepper to taste
>   Juice of 1 lemon
> 10 sprigs fresh thyme
> 6 sprigs fresh rosemary
> 6 sprigs fresh sage
> 16 shallots, peeled and left whole
> 6 cloves garlic, unpeeled
> 1/2 cup white wine

1. Preheat the oven to 400°.

2. Rub the inside of the chicken with salt and pepper and lemon juice. Fill the cavity with half of the fresh herbs. Truss the bird firmly with kitchen string.

3. Put the bird, breast side up, in a shallow heavy roasting pan. (I do not use a rack because it interferes with the cooking of the vegetables.) Put the pan in the middle of the oven and roast for 15 minutes.

4. After 15 minutes, put the shallots and garlic around the chicken. Add most of the remaining herbs to the pan, leaving a few for decoration. Pour the white wine over the shallots and garlic and return the pan to the oven. Roast for another 45 minutes. To test for doneness, pierce the thickest part of the thigh with a sharp knife. The juices should run clear.

5. Arrange the bird on a heated serving platter and distribute the shallots and garlic around it. Decorate with remaining herbs and serve.

Pears Baked in Cream

SERVES 4

> 2 tablespoons (1/4 stick) unsalted
>   butter
> 2 tablespoons sugar
> 2 Bosc or Bartlett pears, unpeeled,
>   halved and cored
> 1/2 cup heavy cream

1. Preheat oven to 400°. Butter a shallow baking dish with 1 tablespoon butter and sprinkle 1 tablespoon sugar over the bottom.

2. Put the pears, cut side down, in the dish. Sprinkle with remaining sugar and dot with butter.

3. Bake for 10 minutes. Pour the cream over the pears and return to the oven for 20 minutes more. Serve warm.

Index

Acorn Squash, Sesame Chicken and
  Vegetables in, 124–25
Apple(s)
  and Cheese, 161
  Chunks, Sautéed, 169
  Pie, Old-Fashioned Bottom Crust, 125
  -Raspberry Crumble, 129
  Sauerkraut with, 57
  Tarts, Paper-Thin, 65
  Thyme-Sautéed Pork Chops with Slices
    of, 104–5
Applesauce, Quick, 200
Apricots
  Baked, 121
  Custard with Golden Raisins and, 205
Artichokes, with Lemon Butter, 68
Arugula and Cherry Tomatoes, Salad of,
  121
Asparagus, Steamed, 16
  with Orange Butter, 40
Avocado with Warm Tomato and Basil
  Vinaigrette, 49

Bananas, Baked, with Rum and Butter, 53
Basil
  Mussels with Pesto, 148–49
  Sliced Tomatoes with Mozzarella and,
    77
  and Tomato Vinaigrette, Avocado with
    Warm, 49
Beans
  Flageolets and Red Runner, 17
  Lima, and Radicchio Salad, 153
Beef
  Carpaccio with Caper-Parsley Sauce, 80
  Grilled Fillet of, with Black Peppercorns,
    188
  Liver with Sage, 216
  Pan-Fried Fillet of, 164
  Steak with Béarnaise Sauce, Broiled, 172
Beet(s)
  Purée of, 161
  -Zucchini Soup, 104
Bibb Lettuce Salad with Grilled Brie on
  French Bread, 124
Blackberry Fool, 17
Boston Lettuce Salad, 29
Bread
  French
    Grilled Brie on, Bibb Lettuce Salad
      with, 124
    Pan-Roasted, 29
  Garlic, Hot, 21
  Italian, Whole-Wheat, with Herb Butter,
    157
  Muffins, Gayla's Orange-Raisin,
    88–89
  Oatmeal Shortbread, 177
Brie, Grilled, on French Bread with Bibb
  Lettuce Salad, 124
Broccoli
  Angel Hair with, 20
  Rabe, Braised Escarole and, 21
  Soup, 152
Brownies, Chocolate Chocolate-Chip, 201

Brussels Sprouts
  with Cream, 145
  in Warm Salad of Winter Vegetables,
    177
Butter Lettuce, Baby Peas and, 64

Cabbage
  -Leek Soup, 212
  Slaw, Three-, 140
Cake, Walnut Pound, Simple, 141
Carpaccio with Caper-Parsley Sauce, 80
Carrot(s)
  Braised Young, 164
  with Cream, 69
  and Mandarin Orange Salad, 213
  in Warm Salad of Winter Vegetables,
    177
Cassis
  Sorbet, 185
  Syrup, Strawberries with, 61
Cheese. See also Brie; Goat Cheese;
    Mozzarella; Parmesan; Stilton
  Apples and, 161
  Exceptional, 189
  for Individual Pizzas, 48
Cherry(-ies)
  Bing
    Iced, Cookies and, 97
    in Fresh Fruit Salad, 117
  Sour, Clafouti, 89
Chicken
  Crusty Mustard, 144
  Herb-Roasted, with Baked Shallots, 221
  Mahogany Fried, 204
  Paillard, 32
  Saffron-Broiled, 52
  Salad, with Snow Peas and Water
    Chestnuts, 88
  Sesame, and Vegetables in Acorn
    Squash, 124
Chicory, Curly
  Salad, 160
    Escarole, Kirby Cucumbers, and, 128
    with Poached Egg and Lardons, 45
    Winter Greens and, 56
  Sautéed in Olive Oil and Garlic, 189
Chocolate
  Cake Trifles, Individual, 29
  Chocolate-Chip Brownies, 201
  Ganache, Hot, Vanilla Ice Cream with,
    137
  Mousse
    Minted, 113
    Tart, Jane's, 165
  Soufflé, 209
Clafouti, Sour Cherry, 89
Clams
  Littleneck, on the Half Shell, 120
  in Seafood Salad, 60
  in Steamed Shellfish with Herbs, 92
Compote, Dried Fruit, 45
Corn on the Cob, Roasted, 76
Crabs, Soft-Shell, 100, 101
Cranberry Kuchen, 145
Crème Fraîche, Blackberry Fool with, 17
Crêpes, Grand Marnier, 173
Cucumbers
  Kirby, Salad of Escarole and Chicory
    and, 128
  Salad, 113

Custard with Apricots and Golden
  Raisins, 205

Daiquiri, Frozen Pineapple, 108
Desserts. See Cake; individual fruits;
    Chocolate; Ice Cream; Sorbet
Duck, Grilled Breast of, 160

Egg(s). See also Frittata; Omelette
  Poached, Frisée Salad with Lardons and,
    45
Eggplant
  with Scallions, 101
  Tian of Potatoes, Zucchini, Whole Garlic
    and, 144–45
Endive
  Grilled, 189
  and Hot Walnuts, Salad of, 25
  and Red Onion, Salad of, 41
Escarole
  Braised Broccoli Rabe and, 21
  and Pancetta, Hot Salad of, 33
  Salad with Chicory and Kirby
    Cucumbers, 128
  in Salad of Winter Greens, 56

Fennel
  Halibut with, 84
  Pan-Sautéed Potatoes and, 28
  Pork Chops with, 136–37
  Salad with Red Onion and Sun-Dried
    Tomatoes, 53
Figs
  with Prosciutto, 72
  Stuffed with Raspberries, 93
Fish. See also Halibut; Red Snapper; Sole;
    Trout
  to grill, 95
Flageolets and Red Runner Beans, 17
Frisée Salad with Poached Egg and
  Lardons, 45
Frittatas, 119, 120
Fruit. See also specific fruits
  Compote, Dried, 45
  Salad, Fresh, 117

Ginger
  Butterscotch Sauce, Ice Cream with
    Homemade Candied, 153
  Pear Soup, 140
  -Soy Sauce, for Steamed Shellfish with
    Herbs, 92
Goat Cheese
  Balls Rolled in Herbs and Spices, 189
  with Salad, Baked, 169
Grand Marnier
  Crêpes, 173
  Zabaglione with, 69
Grapefruit
  Sole and, 196–97
  and Spinach Salad, Ruby Red, 97
Green Beans (String Beans)
  Baby, Tomatoes Stuffed with, 93
  in Salade Nicoise à la Middlefield,
    116–17
  Sautéed, 157

Halibut, with Fennel, 84
Ham. *See also* Prosciutto
    Steak, Oven-Braised, 200
Herb(ed). *See also* Basil; Sage; Tarragon;
        Thyme
    Butter, Whole-Wheat Italian Bread with,
        157
    Crust, Rack of Baby Lamb with, 16
    -Flavored Root Vegetables, 205
    -Mustard Butter, Grilled Veal Chops
        with, 24
    -Roasted Chicken with Baked Shallots,
        221
    Steamed Shellfish with, 92

Ice, Tequila, Papayas with, 181
Ice Cream. *See also* Sorbet
    with Homemade Candied Ginger
        Butterscotch Sauce, 153
    with Hot Chocolate Ganache, 137
    Orange, with Black Raspberry Sauce, 49
    with Sambuca, 21

Jerusalem Artichokes, Braised Scallions
        and, 217

Kielbasa, Simmered in Beer and Onions,
        176

Lamb
    Chops with Mint Butter, 132
    Rack of Baby, with Herb Crust, 16
    Roast Leg of, with Pan-Roasted
        Vegetables, 44
Leek(s)
    Blackened, and Red Onions, 24
    -Cabbage Soup, 212
Lettuce(s). *See individual lettuces*
Lima Bean, and Radicchio Salad, 153
Liver, Beef, with Sage, 216
Lobster, with Linguine, Spicy, 72

Mandarin Orange and Carrot Salad, 213
Mangoes
    with Prosciutto, 72
    Sliced, Indian Style, 133
Melon
    Balls and Strawberries in Bourbon, 77
    with Prosciutto, 72
Mint(ed), Butter, Lamb Chops with, 132
Mousse, Chocolate
    Minted, 113
    Tart, Jane's, 165
Mozzarella
    Pizzas with, 48
    Sliced Tomatoes with Basil and, 77
Muffins, Gayla's Orange-Raisin,
        88–89
Mushrooms
    Porcini, Risotto with, 32
    Ravioli with Sugar Snap Peas and, 61
    and Spinach Salad, 184
    Wild, Omelette with, 28
Mussels
    with Pesto, 148–49
    in Seafood Salad, 60
    in Steamed Shellfish with Herbs, 92

Oatmeal Shortbread, 177
Omelettes. *See also* Frittata
    with Wild Mushrooms, 28
Orange(s)
    Butter, Steamed Asparagus with, 40
    Mandarin, and Carrot Salad, 213
    -Raisin Muffins, Gayla's, 88–89
    in Red Wine, 33
Orzo with Sautéed Onions, 208
Oyster(s)
    with Pink Butter, 184
    Sandwiches, Fried, 212

Paillard, Chicken, 32
Pancakes, Potato, 200–201
Pancetta and Escarole, Hot Salad of, 33
Papayas
    with Prosciutto, 72
    with Tequila Ice, 181
Parmesan
    Red Pepper Pasta with Red Pepper Strips
        and, 37
    Tortellini with Butter and, 80
Pasta
    Angel Hair with Broccoli, 20
    Buckwheat Noodles, Cold, 109
    Fettuccine
        with Smoked Salmon and Fresh Peas,
            197
        with Tomato Sauce, 149
        Tossed with Butter and Cream, 217
        with Uncooked Tomato Sauce, 156
    fresh, about, 36
    Lobster with Linguine, Spicy, 72
    Orzo with Sautéed Onions, 208
    Ravioli, with Mushrooms and Sugar
        Snap Peas, 61
    Red Pepper, with Red Pepper Strips and
        Parmesan, 37
    Rotelle with Bacon and Sautéed
        Walnuts, 185
    Spicy Sesame Noodles, 100–101
    Tortellini, with Butter and Parmesan
        Cheese, 80
Pea(s)
    Baby, and Butter Lettuce, 64
    Fettucine with Smoked Salmon and
        Fresh, 197
    Ravioli with Mushrooms and, 61
    Sautéed, 73
    Soup with Croutons, Fresh, 52
    Sugar Snap
Peaches
    with Brown Sugar and Cognac, Sliced,
        157
    and Plums in Lime Juice, 81
Pear(s)
    Baked in Cream, 221
    Soup, Ginger, 140
    Watercress Salad with Blue Cheese and
        Julienne, 13
    Wine-Poached, with Black Currant
        Sauce, 193
Peppers, Red (Bell)
    Pasta, with Red Pepper Strips and
        Parmesan, 37
    to roast, 147
    Roasted, 148
    Soup, 180
Pesto, Mussels with, 148–49

Pheasant, Roast, 152
Pie, Apple, Old-Fashioned Bottom-Crust,
        125
Pineapple
    and Coconut Curls, Fresh, 41
    Daiquiri, Frozen, 108
Pizzas, Individual, 47, 48
Plums
    Baked Whole Green, 73
    and Peaches in Lime Juice, 81
Pommes Anna, 164
Pork Chops
    Caramelized, with Walnuts and Raisins,
        40
    with Fennel, 136–37
    Thyme-Sautéed, with Apple Slices,
        104–5
Potato(es)
    Baked, 172
        Foil-Baked New Potatoes, 188
    French Fried, 132
    Pancakes, 200–201
    Pan-Sautéed Fennel and, 28
    Pommes Anna, 164
    Slices Fried in Olive Oil, 161
    Sweet, Mashed, 220
    Tian of Zucchini, Eggplant, Whole Garlic
        and, 144–45
    Tian of Zucchini, Tomatoes, and, 129
    Warm, on Lettuce, 192–93
    in Warm Salad of Winter Vegetables,
        177
Pound Cake, Simple Walnut, 141
Prosciutto, Melon with, 72

Rack of Baby Lamb with Herb Crust, 16
Radicchio
    Grilled, 189
    Salad, Lima Bean and, 153
Raspberry(-ies)
    -Apple Crumble, 129
    Black Raspberry Sauce, Orange Ice
        Cream with, 49
    and Cream, 105
    Figs Stuffed with, 93
    to freeze, 127
    in Fresh Fruit Salad, 117
    Vinaigrette, for Watercress Salad with
        Julienne Pears and Blue Cheese,
        136
Red Snapper
    Baked in Parchment, 112–13
    Grilled with Tarragon Butter, 96
Rhubarb, Stewed, 25
Rice
    Baked, 65
    Green, 84
    Risotto with Porcini, 32
    Wild, 41

Saffron-Broiled Chicken Quarters, 52
Sage
    Beef Liver with, 216
    Pan-Sautéed Trout Stuffed with, 36
Salad
    of Arugula and Cherry Tomatoes, 121
    Avocado with Warm Tomato and Basil
        Vinaigrette, 49
    Baked Goat Cheese with, 169
    Bibb Lettuce, with Grilled Brie on French
        Bread, 124

Boston Lettuce, 29
Carrot and Mandarin Orange, 213
Chicken, with Snow Peas and Water
        Chestnuts, 88
Chicory, 160
Cucumber, 113
of Endive and Hot Walnuts, 25
of Endive and Red Onion, 41
of Escarole, Chicory, and Kirby
        Cucumbers, 128
of Escarole and Pancetta, Hot, 33
Fennel, with Red Onion and Sun-Dried
        Tomatoes, 53
Frisée (Curly Chicory), with Poached Egg
        and Lardons, 45
Fruit, Fresh, 117
Lima Bean and Radicchio, 153
Niçoise à la Middlefield, 116–17
Seafood, 60
Spinach and Mushroom, 184
Spinach and Ruby Red Grapefruit, 97
Three-Cabbage Slaw, 140
of Tomatoes with Mozzarella and Basil,
        77
Tomato
    with Red Onion and Fresh Thyme, 85
    Stuffed with Baby String Beans, 93
    Watercress, with Julienne Pears and
        Blue Cheese, 136
of Winter Greens, 56
of Winter Vegetables, Warm, 177
of Young Lettuces, 105
Salad dressing. See Vinaigrette
Salmon, Smoked, Fettuccine with Fresh
        Peas and, 197
    Steaks, Broiled, 64
Sandwiches
    Fried Oyster, 212
    Smoked Turkey and Stilton, 141
Sauce
    Béarnaise, Broiled Steak with, 172
    Black Butter, Sole with Capers and, 128
    Black Currant, Wine-Poached Pears
        with, 193
    Black Raspberry, Orange Ice Cream
        with, 49
    Caper-Parsley, Carpaccio with, 80
    Ginger Butterscotch, Ice Cream with
        Homemade Candied, 153
    Ginger-Soy, for Steamed Shellfish with
        Herbs, 92
    Raspberry, for Figs Stuffed with
        Raspberries, 93
    Tomato, Uncooked, Fettucine with, 156
Sauerkraut with Apples, 57
Sausages
    Kielbasa Simmered in Beer and
        Onions, 176
    Wurst Platter, 57
Scallops
    Sautéed with Scallions, 156
    in Seafood Salad, 60
    in Steamed Shellfish with Herbs, 92
Seafood Salad, 60
Sesame Chicken and Vegetables in Acorn
        Squash, 124–25
Sesame Noodles, Spicy, 100–101
Shallots
    Baked, Herb-Roasted Chicken with, 221
Shellfish. See also individual shellfish
    in Seafood Salad, 60

Steamed, with Herbs, 92
Shortbread, Oatmeal, 177
Shrimp
    Chinoise, 108
    in Seafood Salad, 60
    in Steamed Shellfish with Herbs, 92
    Tortillas, 181
Slaw, Three-Cabbage, 140
Smoked Salmon, Fettuccine with Fresh
        Peas and, 197
Smoked Turkey and Stilton Sandwiches,
        141
Snow Peas, Chicken Salad with Water
        Chestnuts and, 88
Sole
    with Black Butter and Capers, 128
    and Grapefruit, 196–97
    Wrapped in Spinach, Fillet of, 192
Sorbet
    Cassis, 185
    Espresso, 149
Sorrel, Soup, Cold, 112
Soufflé
    Chocolate, 209
    Spinach, 168
Soup
    Beet-Zucchini, 104
    Broccoli, 152
    Cabbage-Leek, 212
    Ginger Pear, 140
    Pea, with Croutons, 52
    Red Pepper, 180
    Sorrel, Cold, 112
    Tomato, Tuscan, 81
Spinach
    Fillet of Sole Wrapped in, 192
    and Garlic, Pan-Sautéed, 173
    and Mushroom Salad, 184
    and Ruby Red Grapefruit Salad, 97
    Soufflé, 168
Squabs, Grilled Butterflied, 76
Squash. See Acorn Squash; Summer
        Squash; Zucchini
Steak with Béarnaise Sauce, Broiled, 172
Stilton, Sandwiches, Smoked Turkey and,
        141
Strawberry(-ies)
    with Cassis Syrup, 61
    and Melon Balls in Bourbon, 77
    Tarts, 85
Sugar Snap Peas, Sautéed, 73
Summer Squash, with Sun-Dried
        Tomatoes, 96–97
Sweet Potatoes, Mashed, 220

Tarragon, Butter, Grilled Red Snapper
        with, 96
Tart(s)
    Apple, Paper-Thin, 65
    Chocolate Mousse, Jane's, 165
    Strawberry, 85
Thyme
    Salad of Tomato, Red Onion, and, 85
    -Sautéed Pork Chops with Apple Slices,
        104–5
Tomato(es)
    and Basil Vinaigrette, Warm, Avocado
        with, 49
    Broiled, 133
    Concasse, Fettuccine with, 149

with Mozzarella and Basil, 77
Salad
    of Arugula and Cherry Tomatoes, 121
    with Red Onion and Fresh Thyme, 85
Sauce, Uncooked, Fettucine with, 156
Soup, Tuscan, 81
Stuffed with Baby String Beans, 93
Sun-Dried
    Fennel Salad with Red Onion and, 53
    Summer Squash with, 86
Tian of Zucchini, Potatoes, and, 129
Tortillas, Shrimp, 181
Trifles, Chocolate Cake, Individual, 29
Trout, Stuffed with Sage, Pan-Sautéed, 36
Turkey, Smoked, and Stilton Sandwiches,
        141
Turnips
    Baby, 16–17
    Dauphinoise, 137

Veal
    Chops, Grilled with Mustard-Herb
        Butter, 24
    Piccata, 208
    Scallopine alla Marsala, 68
    scallops, about, 67
Vegetables. See individual vegetables
Vinaigrettes
    Balsamic Vinegar, 56
    Creamy Mustard, 121
    with Grand Marnier, 213
    Honey Mustard, 160
    Light, 29
    Raspberry, 136
    Rich, 93
    for Salade Niçoise à la Middlefield,
        116–17
    for Seafood Salad, 60
    for Tomato, Red Onion, and Fresh
        Thyme Salad, 85
    Warm, for Frisée Salad with Poached Egg
        and Lardons, 45
    for Warm Potatoes on Lettuce, 192–93
    Warm Tomato and Basil, Avocado with,
        49

Watercress
    Salad with Julienne Pears and Blue
        Cheese, 136
    Sautéed, 165
Watermelon, Iced, 109
Wurst Platter, 57

Zabaglione with Grand Marnier, 69
Zucchini
    -Beet Soup, 104
    Grated, 209
    Tian of Potatoes, Eggplant, Whole Garlic
        and, 144–45
    Tian of Tomatoes, Potatoes and, 129

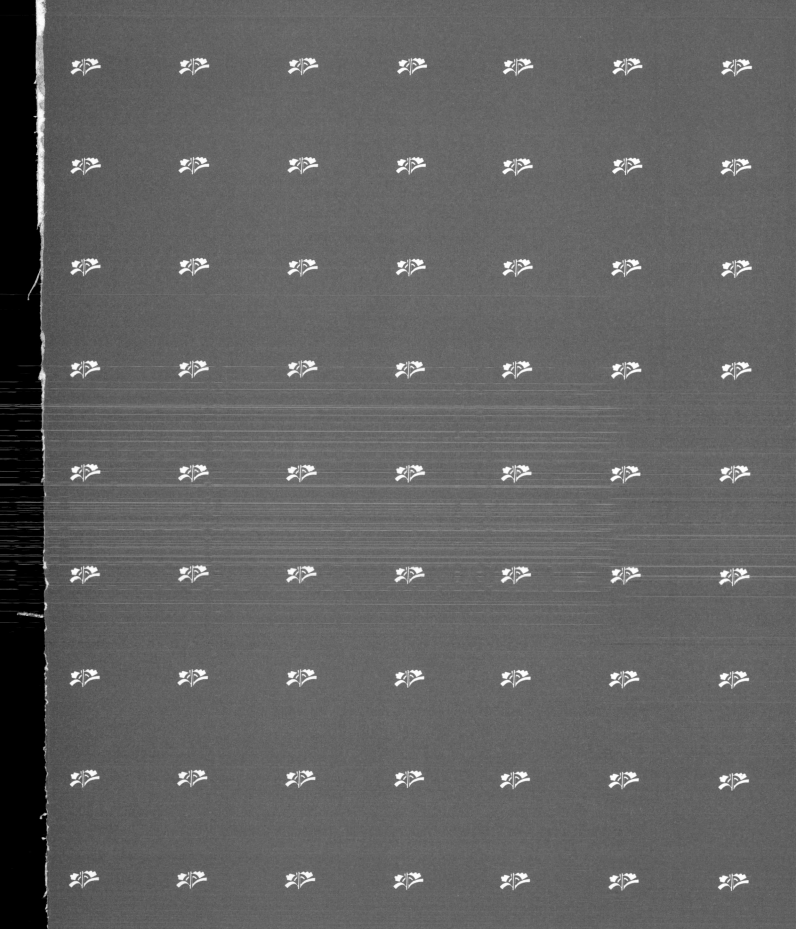